Physical Char[acteristics of the] Tibeta[n Mastiff]

(from the American Ke[nnel Club)

© 2005 American Tibetan Mastiff Association

MW00991050

MAIN LIBRARY
ST. CLAIR COUNTY LIBRARY SYSTEM

Topline: Straight and level between withers and croup.

Tail: Medium to long, but not reaching below hock joint; well feathered. Set high on line with top of back.

WITHDRAWN

Hindquarters: Powerful, muscular, with all parts being moderately angulated. The hocks are strong, well let down (approximately one-third the overall length of the leg) and perpendicular.

Coat: Double-coated, with fairly long, thick coarse guard hair, with heavy soft undercoat in cold weather which becomes rather sparse in warmer months. Hair is fine but hard, straight and stand-off.

Proportion: Slightly longer than tall.

Color: Black, brown and blue/grey, all with or without tan markings, and various shades of gold.

Size: Dogs—minimum of 26 inches at the withers. Bitches—minimum of 24 inches at the withers.

JUL - 2007

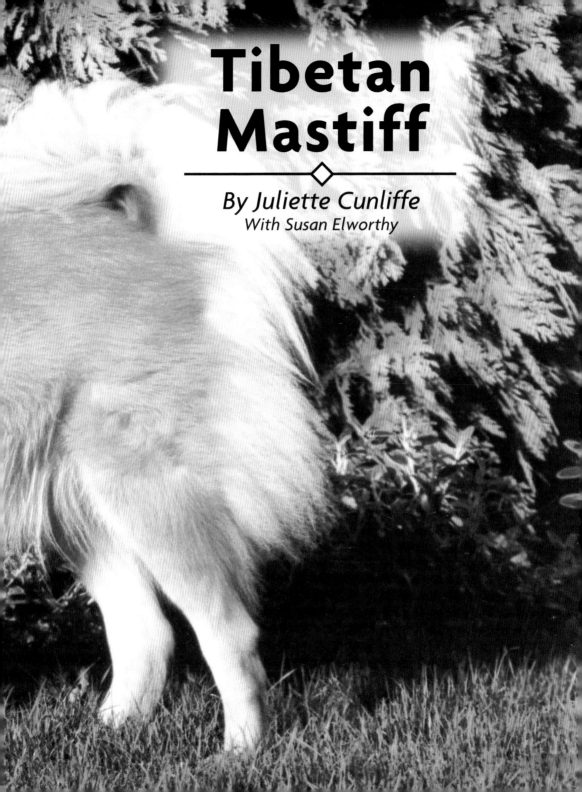

Tibetan Mastiff

By Juliette Cunliffe

With Susan Elworthy

Contents

Training Your Tibetan Mastiff 94

Begin with the basics of training the puppy and adult dog. Learn the principles of house-training, introduce your TM to his collar and leash and progress to the basic commands. Learn positive-reinforcement techniques and consider the TM's unique temperament in your dog's lesson plan.

Healthcare of Your Tibetan Mastiff 115

By Lowell Ackerman DVM, DACVD
Become your dog's healthcare advocate and a well-educated canine keeper. Select a skilled and able veterinarian. Discuss pet insurance, vaccinations and infectious diseases, the neuter/spay decision and a sensible, effective plan for your TM's parasite control, including fleas, ticks and worms.

Showing Your Tibetan Mastiff 140

Step into the center ring and find out about the world of showing pure-bred dogs. Here are the basics of conformation showing with the AKC, UKC and various rare-breed organizations, including how shows are organized and what's required for your dog to become a champion. Also learn about AKC and UKC obedience trials.

KENNEL CLUB BOOKS® TIBETAN MASTIFF
ISBN: 1-59378-287-X

Copyright © 2007 • Kennel Club Books® • A Division of BowTie, Inc.
40 Broad Street, Freehold, NJ 07728 USA
Cover Design Patented: US 6,435,559 B2 • Printed in South Korea

All rights reserved. No part of this book may be reproduced in any form, by photostat, scanner, microfilm, xerography or any other means, or incorporated into any information retrieval system, electronic or mechanical, without the written permission of the copyright owner.

Library of Congress Cataloging-in-Publication Data
Cunliffe, Juliette.
    Tibetan mastiff / By Juliette Cunliffe.
        p. cm. -- (A comprehensive owner's guide ; 351)
    ISBN 1-59378-287-X
    1.   Tibetan mastiff.   I. Title.
SF429.T48C86 2007
636.73--dc22   2006023018
        10 9 8 7 6 5 4 3 2 1

Photography by: Ashbey Photography by Dave McCurley, Paulette Braun, Carolina Biological Supply, Juliette Cunliffe, Isabelle Français, Karen Giles, Stephen Hall, Carol Ann Johnson, Bill Jonas, Dr. Dennis Kunkel, Tam C. Nguyen, Phototake, Jean Claude Revy, Sanne Rutloh, Jay Singh, Christina Timbury, Michael Trafford and Alice van Kempen.

Illustrations by Patricia Peters.

Special acknowledgements to the following: Robyn Allwright, American Kennel Club, Urve Arik (Status Benevoles), Jarmila Bendova (Sundari), Canadian Kennel Club, Canadian Livestock Registration Corporation, David Chambers (Bytesizephoto.com), Mark C. Denk & Laurel Cain-Denk, DVM (FlashPoint), Richard W. Eichhorn (Drakyi), Susan Elworthy (Everest North), Brenda Flett (Dacksville), Sheila Frank (Legend), Ave Frischer (Ay-Yangadoo), Mr. Andreas Gerber, Carol Gordon (Kachar), Gabriele Gruenwald (Gongbo), Gail Harrison, Paul Hawa, Jeff & Judy Hite, Eric Holliday (Chorten's), Laney Humphrey (Jumla), Ray & Linda Larsen (Drakyi), Audrey Lee (Aujudon), Wayne Scot Lukas, Eva Marton (Sengkhri), Barbara and Ian McLuskey (Red Dog), Florence Morris (Kodari), Steve & Linda Nash (Ausables), Dan Nechemias & Lois Claus (Dawa), Sabrina Novarra (Shanghai), Susan Ochsenbein (Himalaya), Jane Otterud (Durettos), J.R. and Betty Jo Parsons (Hardin Valley), Debbie Parsons (Dreamcatcher), Diane and Karri Phillips, Dr. Charles Radcliffe (Timberline), Ann Rohrer (Langtang), Michele Santorini, Irma Schreuder (Lafahhs), Jeff Sera & Corinne Foster, Blanka Slobodjan (Od Rumcajse a Manky), Martha Hamilton Snyder, Lei Song, Lyse Stormont (Stormnangels), Angela Tendermann (Chenporewa) and Efrain Valle (Drakyi).

Preface

Rick Eichhorn with Drakyi Shanghai ("Shang"), a large mastiffy bitch.

With the success of the favorably received first edition of Juliette Cunliffe's *Tibetan Mastiff*, and when the opportunity arose to review and contribute to this revised and expanded second edition, I was happy to accept the invitation. My 30 years of involvement researching breed history, developing the signature Drakyi mastiff type and owning, judging and exhibiting Tibetan Mastiffs from the widest variety of international bloodlines has given me a significant and comprehensive perspective on the development of the breed in the US and abroad, central to the thriving profile in the world today. I am thankful for the opportunity to feature some outstanding examples of the breed in this book from my personal photo archives, and also thankful for the breeders from around the world who have so generously offered photos of their own dogs, with every effort made to give credit where credit is due. Thank you!

Multi-Ch. Formosa-Drakyi Simba ("Simba") is foundational and the archetype for Drakyi Tibetan Mastiffs.

Drakyi Leeloo ("Leeloo") is a typey mature TM female.

This enhanced 2007 edition of *Tibetan Mastiff* marks the breed's debut in the American Kennel Club's Working Group. This book provides a look into the breed's origins, the breeders and bloodlines behind US and Canadian TMs, the TM's characteristics and the official standards for the breed, and also provides guidelines for the proper care and training of a Tibetan Mastiff puppy. For those interested in conformation showing and obedience competition, advice is offered on how to prepare your TM for these events.

Juliette Cunliffe is well known for her experience and expertise with Tibetan breeds, her many travels to their native lands and from her volumes of insightful publications devoted to the breeds from the "Roof of the World." That perspective, along with my section on US history and contributions from co-author Susan Elworthy throughout the book, including a detailed look at the development of the breed in Canada, provides a volume that is an informative and substantive introduction to the breed for new fanciers, as well as a welcomed addition to any established Tibetan Mastiff library.

The Tibetan Mastiff has made a powerful return to the world of pure-bred dogs after its near-demise a half-century ago in occupied Tibet, and the breeders and dogs featured in these pages are representative of the efforts of the international community of Tibetan Mastiff devotees working on the breed's behalf.

Richard W. Eichhorn
Drakyi Tibetan Mastiffs
www.tibetanmastiff.com

Timberline Barni Drakyi ("Barnes") is a golden Simba grandson who represents generations of quality from his pedigree.

Drakyi Titus Lukas. A classic head study of a great dog, showing the fully developed mane, a breed characteristic.

Rick with World Ch. Drakyi Senge Sundari ("Senge") in a celebratory moment after Senge's Best of Breed win at the 2003 World Dog Show under breed-specialist judge Christofer Habig.

TIBETAN MASTIFF

ORIGIN OF THE BREED

One could not talk about the Tibetan Mastiff, nor truly try to understand the Tibetan Mastiff, without knowing the general history of the breed. Respect for and understanding of this breed are crucial for successful ownership.

According to pictures, stone carvings, unearthed bones and writings, the Tibetan Mastiff is of ancient lineage (possibly as old as 3000 BC) and originates from Tibet. The physical geography of Tibet has made for a natural pure-bred landrace. The Tibetan Mastiff has played a part in the development of the Newfoundland, Bernese

An ink and color on silk illustration from the Ch'ing Dynasty titled *One of the Ten Prized Dogs, named Ts'ang-ni.* This is the first color depiction of a TM ever done (brown and tan color). Circa 1750 by Giuseppe Castiglione in China.

Mountain Dog, Komondor, St. Bernard, Neapolitan Mastiff, Dogue de Bordeaux and Mastiff as well as many other large livestock-guardian breeds.

The Tibetan Mastiff is a veritable "king" of dogs with an ancient background; indeed, it has been said by some that this is possibly the very oldest of all large dogs. The Tibetan Mastiff gained almost legendary status over the centuries, as few Westerners had ever seen the breed, but stories about them were told by early travelers to Tibet.

In 1271 the renowned traveler Marco Polo embarked on a journey that made history. It was from his account of his travels that we have the first documented evidence of the great dog of Tibet. He first encountered such dogs in China's Szechuan province, where they accompanied Tibetan traders. He recounted that every man on a journey took a couple of these dogs with him, as they were so bold and fierce that two could attack a "lion." Here, though, I should clarify that the "lions" that he mentioned were actually tigers.

It has perplexed many that Polo described these dogs as being "the size of donkeys." It should be appreciated that donkeys in that region are much smaller than those we know in the West. However, the author has it on good authority that there are many Tibetan Mastiffs in Tibet that are much larger than those with which we are now familiar. Several different Tibetan people have described these dogs as standing about 36 inches (91.5 cms) high at the shoulder, some 10 inches (25.5 cms) taller than the minimum height required for a male according to the English Kennel Club's breed standard.

Tibet is known fondly as "The Roof of the World," a mystical country with a barren landscape. The country's dogs, like its people, have to be able to deal with extremes of temperature, fiercely bright light and high altitude, the majority living between 10,500 and 16,400 feet (3,200 and 5,000 meters). All the dogs of this region have to be sufficiently hardy to survive in the inhospitable terrain. Certainly for the Tibetan Mastiff, living as it has done in isolated communities, it has been a matter of "survival of the fittest." Weak dogs would simply not have been reared beyond puppyhood.

Historically, the Tibetan Mastiff's work has been primarily to defend his people and territory. In Tibet, he defended pastoral nomads, villages (especially women and children), caravans and monasteries from thieves (and perceived

strangers like foreigners). The TM has also had a place in livestock-predator control as well, protecting yaks (known as "the blacks") and goats or sheep (known as "the whites") from wolves and leopards. Occasionally, it is said that the Tibetan Mastiff was also used as a salt carrier.

As the centuries passed, the British sent missions to Tibet in the hope of establishing trade relations and in 1774 we have another vivid description of the breed. This came from George Bogle, who was sent to

This means "Tibetan Mastiff" in Tibetan.

NOT THE ONLY ONE

In the Himalayas, Tibetan Mastiffs are found in the more agile mountain type and the more mastiff-like monastery type, but are not the only large dogs found there. Others include the Bangara Mastiff and the Bhotia, sometimes also called the Himalayan Sheepdog. Yet another is the Kyi Apso (formerly Apso Do-Kyi), a large, shaggy guard dog from the area around Tibet's Mount Kailash. The Shakhi (or Sha-Kyi), or Tibetan Hunting Dog, is another magnificent but rare breed, with a shorter coat.

A drawing from the early 19th century depicts an old-time Tibetan Mastiff, which was believed to be very ferocious.

They were used as guardians of the home; however, these dogs were so aggressive that it was unsafe to approach them unless their keepers were nearby. The report of this mission is particularly absorbing, for in Bhutan a row of wooden cages is described, in each of which was a massive dog, very similar to those that had been seen in Tibet.

THE 19th CENTURY

During the 19th century there was an increasing flow of British people to Asia. Nepal had become a British dependency, and more than one zoologist or adventurer found their way into this magical country, from where they sent reports on the dogs they had seen. In 1845 Joseph Dalton Hooker, who also went into southern Tibet, wrote of his meeting with a noble-looking black Tibetan Mastiff. Its gloriously bushy tail was thrown over its back in a majestic sweep, and around its neck it wore a thick collar of scarlet wool. This is still a traditional ornament on

Tibet by Warren Hastings, the first Governor General of Bengal. The dogs he saw were large and "shagged like a lion," and they were extremely fierce. Bogle also gave us an insight into the manner in which the Tibetan Mastiffs were kept: chained during the day and let loose at night, a tradition that is continued today. After all, the Tibetan Mastiff is a protector and it is sensible to allow him to roam free at night when the household is sleeping, and when both domestic livestock and humans need to be guarded from predators and human intruders.

A second British mission was dispatched to Tibet in 1783 and again from this we learn of the Tibetan Mastiff. On the border of Tibet and Bhutan, two large dogs protected a herd of around 300 yaks. The dogs were apparently huge and not only tremendously fierce but also strong and noisy.

> **BELIEVE IT OR NOT**
> It is believed that Marco Polo was the first Westerner to own a Tibetan Mastiff. So impressed was he by the breed that he had one of his own for protection on his journeys. This dog accompanied him on his homeward-bound journey, though it is not thought likely that the dog could ever have reached Polo's eventual destination in Italy.

various Tibetan mountain dogs and it helps to give them an even more majestic and imposing appearance.

Increasing interest was shown in the breed in the Himalayan regions, and in 1847 Lord Hardinge, who was then Viceroy of India, sent a dog named Bout to Queen Victoria in England. Siring, a black-and-tan male, was brought back to England in 1874 by the prince who later became Edward VII. This magnificent dog became well known, in part because he was exhibited at shows, thereby attracting attention to the breed.

Those intrepid travelers of the 19th century were kind enough to recount their tales in detail, and from these it is easy to pick up various different snippets of information about the Tibetan Mastiff as well as some of its close relatives. We learn that the killing of a dog was a serious matter, resulting in a fine of 25 rupees. This fine could be waived, however, if the dog died as a result of blows on the head, as this was considered proof that the killing was in self defense.

These dogs were described as being enormous beasts; they had heads like those of bears. Several colors were described: black, black and tan or red. However, we should not overlook the fact that some reports referred to smaller mountain dogs of the Himalayas, and we should also remember today that there are not only Tibetan Mastiffs in that mountainous terrain. There

In one of the author's excursions to Tibet, she met this nomad with his Tibetan Mastiff outside the Tashilhumpo Monastery.

are also other large dogs, of different kinds, most rather smaller in stature. Although the dividing line between various breeds in the Himalayan regions can be thin, we must continually take care not to confuse other dogs with the Tibetan Mastiff. Only by being aware of these differences can the Tibetan Mastiff that is preserved in the West be typical of the true breed in its homeland.

THE EARLY 20th CENTURY

As the 19th century moved into the next, the British were increasingly concerned about the safety of their

An engraving dated 1840 showing the Tibetan Mastiff.

The author has encountered many wonderfully helpful Tibetan nomads in her travels to Tibet. This lovely nomad woman posed with her Tibetan Mastiff puppy for the camera.

empire, and in 1903 and 1904 the Younghusband Expedition took place in Tibet. Again, interesting reports of the dogs were sent back, with the comment that often these dogs had a white patch on their chests, suggestive of that on a bear.

THE HOMELAND

The Tibetan Mastiff's homeland, Tibet, is a high table land, the plains around Lhasa being about 2 miles (3.2 kms) above sea level. In size Tibet is equal to France, Germany and Great Britain combined, and temperatures vary considerably. Within the space of a day, temperatures may rise from below freezing to 100°F.

There were also reports of lion-like heads and manes on certain specimens.

Major W. Dougall, who was involved with the Younghusband Expedition in Tibet, acquired the Tibetan Mastiff named Bhotean and brought him back to England. This dog was considered a fine specimen of his breed, the best then ever seen in Great Britain. Major Dougall, who incidentally later sold Bhotean for a high price, clearly had a great interest in the Tibetan Mastiff, and the author feels that his comments about the breed, though lengthy, are well worthy of quotation:

"These wonderfully handsome dogs are now yearly becoming more difficult to obtain…They are, generally speaking, black and bright red tan. They have almost all got a white star or patch on the chest. Bhotean in his own country was considered a particularly fine specimen, and there was nothing like him amongst the others which I saw, which were brought to India on the return of the Thibet Expedition in 1904. He was the long, low type, on very short legs, with great bone, and enormously powerful…His characteristics were many and various. He was essentially a one man's dog. I could do anything with him, but he had an uncontrollable aversion to all strangers (male), but never attempted to attack any child or woman. He was, in consequence, always led at exercise, and, latterly, never allowed loose. At first I

thought he had become quite domesticated, and allowed him to go loose, but with disastrous results. You could not cure him of his fault regarding strangers (men) as his personal enemies. He was an excellent guard, always awake at night and resting during the day. He had a great fondness for puppies and cats, and used invariably to have one or other in his box (loose).

"These dogs can stand any amount of cold, but they cannot endure wet and damp. Their own country being practically rainless, this is perhaps accounted for. The

A Tibetan Mastiff in a typical setting in Tibet, circa 1911. This was one of the early photos upon which familiarity with the breed in the West was based.

MY COUSIN ST. BERNARD

The Tibetan Mastiff and the St. Bernard are both believed to have the same Stone Age progenitor. Indeed, these two mountain breeds, their homelands thousands of miles apart, share many similarities. Author Max Siber documents in 1897 in *Der Tibethund* that in both breeds, "The presence of the fifth and sixth toe should be observed—these are the so-called double wolf claws or double dewclaws."

Bhutans, who use these dogs, are a copper-colored race; they set the same value on them as the Arab does upon his horse. They are used as guards and protectors only, and are in no sense a sheep dog. When the Bhutans come down to the plains to sell their produce the dogs are left behind as guard to their women and children. Also, during the short summer, they are taken to guard the flocks and herds, which travel long distances to forage.

"These dogs have very often a great leather collar on with roughly beaten spikes on it, so that, in the event of a leopard or panther attacking them, they are protected from the fatal grip which these animals always try for on the throat. When the herds are stationary for any time, the natives hobble the dogs, by tying their forelegs together, crossed. As they have excellent noses, and are always on the "qui vive," they soon speak at the *approach of any wild animal or stranger, when they are set loose at once. The only food (flesh) they get is what they kill themselves. The bitches are very hard to get, and in my opinion unless you could breed them and train them from puppyhood in this country, they are not worth the trouble of importing, as you cannot alter the dog's nature, and although perhaps for months he shows no sign of the aggression in him, it is assuredly there, and for no reason or provocation the old hatred of strangers will assert itself, more especially if he happens to be suddenly aroused or startled."*

Dougall goes on to describe Bhotean's journey through India, a journey in which the dog had a railway carriage to himself and effectively cleared the platform at any station where the train stopped and he was exercised. Dougall felt that the breed took about 18 months

> **EARLY ROCK CARVINGS**
> In the Himalayan kingdom of Zanskar there are rock carvings that are believed to be at least 3,000 years old. This, in itself, is interesting, but more so is the fact that they depict dogs of Tibetan Mastiff type in the company of humans.

to acclimatize to weather conditions in England. He also commented that in his opinion they would never live under the conditions at the Zoological Gardens, and how right he was. Sadly, the Tibetan Mastiffs kept there seemed not to have lasted long, such as one brought home by H. R. H. the Prince of Wales in 1906. This dog had his coat shorn while in transit and unfortunately only survived there a few weeks.

Those early imports to Britain created great astonishment and

The famed and well-traveled Tibetan Mastiff Bhotean, who had such a great influence on the modern Tibetan Mastiff.

interest. The land of Tibet was mysterious, and the dogs of the country had a certain mystery about them, too. Encounters with Tibetan Mastiffs in their homeland are exceptionally well recorded. However, it is impossible to do justice to all the many anecdotal images within the confines of this book. Nevertheless, we cannot move forward without commenting on the Hon. Mrs. Irma Bailey's contribution to the breed.

IRMA BAILEY'S OBSERVATIONS

Irma Bailey was the wife of Colonel Eric Bailey, who took part in the Younghusband Expedition. She was much enamored of the Tibetan breeds and later played an active

RARE BLUE HUE
Tibetan Mastiffs that are blue in color (a slate gray) have been little known until fairly recently in the West. However, Max Siber, writing in Switzerland in 1897, said that blue Tibetan Mastiffs with red markings occurred even then, albeit very rarely.

Tibetan Mastiff Shekyar Gyandru, owned by the Hon. Mrs. Eric Bailey, and her two-month-old puppy. This puppy, born in early 1931, was among the first of the breed to be born in Great Britain.

part in their establishment in Britain. She wrote about the breeds in England's *Kennel Gazette*, her articles subsequently appearing in America. She commented on the Tibetan Mastiff's deep-voiced bark and talked of some entirely black ones, owned by the Tashi Lama. Tan markings, she said, were not unusual and "not infrequently red dogs are found in a litter." This latter point is certainly worthy of note, for in Britain in recent decades the subject of color has caused much heated debate. The Hon. Mrs. Bailey, like the author, can confirm that red Tibetan Mastiffs do most certainly exist in their homeland, contrary to what some folk have led others to believe.

Mrs. Bailey also commented that Tibetan Mastiffs seemed quite impervious to the cold, electing to lie out on a patch of snow if one were available, in high winds and freezing temperatures. As she put it, so descriptively, "In Tibet they are not active dogs except when actively carrying out the military

THE BREED NAME

The Tibetan Mastiff is known in FCI countries as Do Khyi. This means "dog you can tie up," but is, in fact, used in Tibet for other breeds besides the Tibetan Mastiff. As it can also be translated as "gate dog," one should appreciate that however endearing the name, "Do Khyi" might just as easily be used to describe any other large dog used for guarding purposes. In Taiwan the breed is called Ao-chen while in China it is known as Zang-ao.

precept that attack is often the best form of defense." She felt that the reason for their ferocity was that they were kept tied up from puppyhood, but noted that they were very affectionate and good-tempered with people they knew.

Colonel and Mrs. Bailey brought some Tibetan Mastiffs back to England with them, along with Lhasa Apsos. Indeed, the couple was to become very influential in the division and clarification of the breed standards for the various Tibetan breeds during the early 1930s.

From historical archives: A Tibetan Mastiff with the collection of animals and birds presented to the Prince of Wales by the Maharaja of Nepal.

THE BREED IN THE UNITED STATES

by Richard W. Eichhorn

The first documented arrival of Tibetan Mastiffs into the United States was in 1958. A request was made in New Delhi at the American Embassy to send a pair of Tibetan Terriers to the US, but what was actually sent to President Eisenhower was a pair of Tibetan Mastiffs! The pair was then given to Senator Harry Darby, who bred them, but the whereabouts of most of the progeny, as well as the fate of the original pair, are unknown.

In 1969 a Tibetan Mastiff was imported into the United States from Nepal. This was a vision shared by and a cooperative effort between Don Messerschmidt (Emodus prefix), Ann Rohrer, Laney Humphrey and Ann Schneider-Olsen. Jumla's Kalu of Jumla (1967–1981) is known as the Tibetan Mastiff foundation dog in the US. He was the first stud dog registered with The Tibetan Mastiff Club (TTMC, later becoming the American Tibetan Mastiff Association) as #001, and was owned by the breed's founder in the US, Ann Rohrer of the Langtang kennel in Pearblossom, California.

Ann Rohrer and Linda Larsen (Dragonquest TMs), founders of the An-Lin strain of Tibetan Mastiff, wrote a short comprehensive study of the TM that was published in the US in 1981. In this they record that two more TMs arrived in the US: St.

Mary's Yullah of Langtang (a bitch from Nepal in 1973) and St. Mary's Kipu of Langtang (a bitch from north of Katmandu, Nepal in

EUROPE AND THE UK

During the 1970s a few imports arrived in Europe from the US, Nepal and India, among them Thandup, Rinki, Saheru, Mirage, Su-chen, Grey King, Rani Sadiya and the famous Tu-bo, bred by Mr. Jay Singh, president of the Nepal Kennel Club. On the Continent, although numbers were not high compared to those of other breeds, the TM was fortunate to have had some exceptionally dedicated breeders who strived to breed truly typical, outstanding dogs. Early influential European kennels included Van Desaal, Chattang, De la tour Chandos, Taiwinds, Gesar, Begero, Krekelberg, Soechavati, Zegse Heide and Yi-dam; in the UK, Rockanor, Qassaba and Farnemoor produced early litters.

Two TMs were imported to Britain in 1981, but sadly both died in quarantine. The next year, two bitches were imported from the US, both in whelp, producing 13 puppies, the dams subsequently returning to the US. Several other Tibetan Mastiffs have been imported to Britain from a number of countries, and though there are still relatively few Tibetan Mastiffs seen at shows in Britain, the breed has had its own classes at Crufts since 1991, with TMs from other countries eligible to compete in the UK via the Pet Passport system.

1975). Jumla's Kalu of Jumla sired the first US-born litters out of Ausables Chang-du in November 1973, Jumla's Michu in January and December 1975, St. Mary's Yullah in February 1975 and St. Mary's Kipu in January and December 1977.

The TM bitch Ausables Chang-du, owned by Ken Summers, became the foundation bitch for the Ausables kennel in New York, owned by Steven and Linda Nash. Puppies produced in her litters by Jumla's Kalu of Jumla (in November 1973) and I Ching (in December 1974) became the foundation for all Ausables pedigrees, with subsequent influences from imports Beisler's Kachook (in November 1976) and Angmo Rajkumri Chattang, known as "The Dutchman" (in December 1981).

Those first US imports were the fulfillment of a dream that began in the 1960s by a group of Americans and others working in Nepal who

This photo from 1958 shows "two jet black Sherpa dogs, ordered by President Eisenhower's special assistant, Thomas Stevens... This rare species of Tibetan Mastiffs are reported to be the first pair ever sent to the United States." Having arrived from Nepal, the dogs were photographed outside a New Delhi, India hospital, where they received inoculations before being flown to the US.

ROAD TO RECOGNITION

The Miscellaneous Class of both the American Kennel Club (AKC) and the Canadian Kennel Club (CKC) are made up of breeds that are registered by the respective organizations in supplemental registries but have not yet received full recognition. In this group, the Tibetan Mastiff Best of Breed winner goes on to compete with the Best of Breed winners from other breeds waiting for full recognition. After almost 30 years of participating in rare-breed events in the US, the Tibetan Mastiff entered the AKC's Miscellaneous Group in January 2005 and then was moved into the AKC's Working Group with full recognition in January 2007.

In Canada the TM entered the CKC's Miscellaneous Group and was registered by the same since early 1994, and eligible to participate in conformation events. Canadian breeders hope for further recognition in the future, allowing the TM to compete for CKC championships.

realized that the Tibetan Mastiff was readily becoming extinct in its native land, a result of the Chinese occupation of Tibet in 1959. The idea for The Tibetan Mastiff Club (TTMC) was also envisioned during this time period; this was an organization devoted to the protection and preservation of this magnificent breed. In 1974 this vision became a reality and TTMC was incorporated. In 1975 the club's registry and studbook were established.

It is estimated that there were approximately 100 Tibetan Mastiffs in America by the end of 1978. TTMC held its first national specialty in October 1979 in conjunction with the California Rare Breed Dog Association. Linda Larsen's Ch. Langtang Gawa Trempa CDX, "Tang," was Best of Breed, and the Nashes' Ch. Ausables

Tibetan nomad women with their Tibetan Mastiff companions on a road in Nepal. The nomads consider the dogs to be part of their families.

Abacus was Best of Opposite Sex. In October 1980, TTMC put on its first independent club-sponsored specialty match, showing their TMs before American Kennel Club (AKC) Working-Group judge Ed Gilbert in Lake Los Angeles, California. This show was held again in 1981 and 1982.

April of 1983 marked an historic Tibetan Mastiff event. TTMC founding officers President Ann Rohrer, Vice President Linda Larsen and Registrar Richard Eichhorn met with the Tibetan Mastiff Club of America's (TMCA) President Steven Nash and Secretary Kristina Sherling and amalgamated TTMC and TMCA to found the American Tibetan Mastiff Association (ATMA). This organization had a new standard and registry that held American- and Canadian-registered Tibetan Mastiffs. The first ATMA national specialty was held in Palmdale, California in October 1, 1983, with Ausables Takkar Dokyi, owner/handled by Richard Eichhorn, taking Best of Breed honors. In 1984 the newly formed ATMA New York/Pennsylvania regional club (NEWPA) held its first specialty in conjunction with the 1984 ATMA national specialty, with national/regional specialty venues then trading off between the East and West Coasts throughout the 1980s and 1990s.

Other Tibetan Mastiff organizations have come and gone, like

The Tibetan Mastiff Club of Southern California (TTMCSC) and People for the Protection of the Tibetan Mastiff (PPTM), while some remain, including the now-independent ATMA regional Pacific Northwest Tibetan Mastiff Association (PNTMA) and the United States Tibetan Mastiff Club (USTMC), to name a few. These groups have modest memberships and sponsor occasional local TM events. Ann Rohrer and Steve Nash both judged for TMCA and PNTMA, with Miss Rohrer presenting a perpetual Nepali prayer stone trophy for PNTMA's Best of Breed; also, a TMCA memorial trophy is awarded in her honor.

Breed founder in the West, Ann Rohrer, with a puppy from her Langtang kennel.

A remarkable photograph of a Tibetan Mastiff with a shorn coat, imported from India by H. R. H. the Prince of Wales in 1906.

Influential and other contributing US kennel names during the 1970s, '80s and '90s included the following (listed as kennel prefix/owner's name): Ausables/Nash, Langtang/Rohrer, Dragonquest/Larsen, Dokyi/Eichhorn, Drakyi (Dragonquest/Dokyi merge), Sierras'/Sherling, Shayri/Pickel, Tai Ching/Adair, Caloosa/Walton, Jamars/Reisinger, Karakorum/Leininger,

CENTER: The author greets a Tibetan nomad walking the road with her Tibetan Mastiff. The Tibetan landscape is no less than breathtaking.

The author photographed this Tibetan Mastiff in its homeland. Note the distinctive red yak-hair collar around the dog's neck.

Stonenail/Steinnagel, Jastone (Jamars/Stonenail merge), I-gors/Goldsmith, Mao T'o Shih/McLemore, Kailas/Brent, Timberline/Radcliffe, Denali/Estep, Shampa/Boget, Hoshen/Young, Kankaa/Engel, Alaska/Nowland, Chang Ku/Wolfe, Funquest/Macy, Shanghai/Novarra, Kachar/Gordon, Himalaya/Ochsenbein, Formosa/Hsieh, Mansata/Gerry, Arctic Sun/Orr, Drukeh/Oviatt, Molosser/Escobedo, HyTyme/

Gabaldon, WuWay/Woltering, Kesang Camp/Bombliss, Braveheart/Hogue, Lionheart/Benson, Sherekhan/Porter, Legend's/Frank and others, who would all make their mark and leave their legacy in US pedigrees. Only a handful of these breeders are still active in the breed today, with influences of select Tibetan exports via Taiwan and China seen in Western bloodlines throughout the 1990s through the present day.

In the mid-1990s, the AKC began a supplemental registry for rare-breed dogs, the Foundation Stock Service (FSS), providing a secure, reliable and reputable avenue to maintain registry records until AKC recognition could be achieved. A subject of great controversy at the time, this, along with political differences, led to divisions within the breed club. The founding ATMA leadership left the club to reorganize and become TMCA, and ATMA continued with new leadership. In 2001, TMCA's membership voted to turn over their registry and stud book to the AKC's FSS, followed in 2002 by ATMA's doing the same, resulting in over 3,000 TMs being entered into the FSS Registry.

TMCA went on with its breed standard and affiliation with the United Kennel Club (UKC), while ATMA was designated as the parent club for the AKC, with the breed

The Canadian Tibetan Mastiff Association
Registration Certificate and Certified Pedigree

TOP: Pedigree of Van Fichtental kennel's foundation dog and the Canadian Tibetan Mastiff Association's #001 dog, Attila v. Fichtental. BOTTOM: Of further interest is that Attila's sire, Jumla's Kalu of Jumla, pictured here with a young friend, is the foundation dog of the breed in the United States.

moving into the AKC's Miscellaneous Class on January 1, 2005. In April 2006, the breed was given the green light for full AKC recognition beginning on January 1, 2007 as part of the Working Group.

THE TM IN CANADA

In Canada, it is thought that a man named Gerald D'Aoust, who also

Mr. Jay Singh, President of the Nepal Kennel Club, posing with one of his Tibetan Mastiffs, is a very close friend of the author who assisted greatly in the research for this book. His breeding is highly influential in the breed and behind most breed members today.

imported Rampour Hounds from India, imported the first Tibetan Mastiffs. Mr. D'Aoust registered the dogs with Agriculture Canada's

A handsome solid black Tibetan Mastiff with her owner in Nepal, photographed by the author.

federally regulated *General Stud and Herd Book* (GSHB) under the breed name Do Khyi. Forty-four Do Khyi were registered in the GSHB by the time they were taken out of the registry on June 20, 1985 due to a change in the rules of eligibility for the GSHB. It is said that Mr. D'Aoust was encouraged by many in the Canadian Kennel Club (CKC) to get the breed fully recognized by the CKC, but due to Mr. D'Aoust's dedication to the health of the breed, he did not believe that he had enough genetic diversity in his stock to avoid health problems that may have occurred had he linebred his stock as Agriculture Canada required.

Another of the known founding breeders in Canada was Oscar Scholz in Thunder Bay, Ontario under the kennel name Van Fichtental; he also started the Canadian Tibetan Mastiff Association (CTMA) in 1977. His foundation pair was a black and tan dog and a black and tan bitch. The dog was bought from Laney Humphrey in 1975, was named Attila v. Fichtental and was registered with the Canadian Tibetan Mastiff Association (CTMA) as #001. He was by TMCA #3 Jumla's Kalu of Jumla (from Nepal) x ATMA #S-0001 Jumla's Michu. The bitch was named Ausables Balu v. Fichtental (call name "Decki") and was CTMA #0002. She was by TMCA #12 Ausables Abacus x TMCA #17 Ausables Acadia, who came from Steve and Linda Nash of Ausables kennel in the US in 1976. Progeny included at least two litters from which he also bred King and Kulla (full brother and sister). From Attila and Ausables Balu v. Fichtental (CTMA #002) came a dog named Dombu v. Fichtental. Mr. Scholz also owned some lines from India that proved to be of poor

A very early photo captioned "The Great Dog of Tibet" has often been considered to depict a Tibetan Mastiff. The author believes that it is more likely a Kyi Apso or Tibetan Bearded Dog, a related Tibetan breed used for hunting and guarding.

quality and were not used in his breeding program. He owned over 15 TMs.

Mr. Scholz had tried to get the breed recognized in Canada with the CKC, but was unsuccessful. His CTMA had been the Canadian registry for the Tibetan Mastiff since 1976 and included the Canadian TM breed standard. It was not officially recognized as a national club in Canada, as Mr. Scholz did

not get enough directors from all of the required provinces of the country. The Maritime Provinces could not be represented, as no TM owners/fanciers were known to live there at the time. Eventually all of those TMs registered with the CTMA were admitted to the ATMA registry.

Upon Mr. Scholz's death, much of his stock went to Bruce and Brenda Flett of Thunder Bay, Ontario to continue his breeding program. To date, there has not been an officially recognized club formed

Historical photo of Ausables Khan, owned by US breed pioneers Steve and Linda Nash of Ausables kennel.

Early breed pioneer in Canada, Gerald D'Aoust.

ABOVE: Bred by Richard Eichhorn and exported to Canada to become the country's first TM champion, this is the beautiful and impressive Drakyi Maharajah, "Shon Shon." RIGHT: Barb McLuskey with Stone (behind) and Tillie (front). Tillie (Atbyrnecliff Goodwill Jamar) was the foundation bitch for Barb and Ian McLuskey's Red Dog kennel and lived to almost 13 years of age.

in Canada, although there has been informal cohesion among breeders and owners. The Canadian Tibetan Mastiff Society was formed in 2001.

The first Tibetan Mastiff Canadian champion was a beautiful black and tan US export, Drakyi Maharajah, known as "Shon Shon." Born in January 1992, Shon Shon (by Ch. Hytyme's Bodashus Buefrd x Ch. Drakyi Mayo Anjin) was exported by breeder Richard Eichhorn of Drakyi Tibetan Mastiffs

One of Canada's foundation bitches, CTMA #002, Ausables Balu v. Fichtental ("Decki").

in California to Michael Yinge of Ontario, who also imported a male from Sierras' Tibetan Mastiffs in the US to add to his several other TMs from his native Taiwan. Shon Shon was sold to Mr. Cliff Byrne of Atbyrnecliff Tibetan Mastiffs in Alymer, Ontario, where he was bred to the foundation bitch Atbyrnecliff Goodwill Jamar ("Tillie," born December 1992). Both Shon Shon and Tillie were eventually sold at four or five years of age to then-new breeders Ian and Barb McLuskey of Red Dog kennel in Everett, Ontario. Over the last 20 years, many imports have come to Canada from Europe, especially France and Belgium, as breeding stock. Most of these have been imported by breeders in Quebec.

The Tibetan Mastiff was added to the CKC's Miscellaneous Class in early 1994. Mr. Cliff Byrne and Ms. Patti Klinkhamer (Tibetan Mastiff owner) made the request to have the breed added to the Miscellaneous Class list and it has been classified as such ever since. In spite of the fact that more and more interest in the breed continues in Canada, the Tibetan Mastiff has remained in the CKC's Miscellaneous Class, which has been extremely frustrating for breeders and exhibitors alike. The first referendum vote that included the Tibetan Mastiff took place in 1997. The Tibetan Mastiff received 18% of the required 25% of votes

At 16 months of age, Everestnorth's Targo Thor ("Thor") was Best of Winners at the 2006 ATMA national speciality. Breeder/owner handled by Sue Elworthy of Canada.

from CKC members and therefore was not granted full recognition at that time. With the AKC's announcement of full recognition of the Tibetan Mastiff in the United States, the CKC and AKC have agreed to let litters born of AKC-registered parents but whelped in Canada to be registered with the AKC until such time as the TM is fully recognized in Canada. The Canadian Tibetan Mastiff breeders anticipate the TM's entering the Working Group in the not-too-distant future.

CHARACTERISTICS OF THE

TIBETAN MASTIFF

WHY THE TIBETAN MASTIFF?
It is only fair, both to the breed and to prospective owners, to say that the Tibetan Mastiff is not the right choice for everyone. This is undoubtedly a unique breed with a very special disposition and temperament. For centuries this strong, independent dog has worked as a guardian for the home and for livestock. So, unless an owner is prepared to understand the breed's mentality and to give proper training, a Tibetan Mastiff should not even be considered.

It is a wonderful breed, and those who love the breed are almost invariably besotted with it. In the right hands, the Tibetan Mastiff can be a well-adjusted dog, capable of giving wonderful companionship. However, problems will arise for owners who do not understand and aren't willing to dedicate themselves to this unique canine.

PERSONALITY
The breed standard clearly states that the Tibetan Mastiff is "aloof and protective." To understand the personality of the breed, it is necessary to look back through history and to appreciate how the dog has been used for centuries in Tibet. Modern lifestyles in the West can in no way be compared with life in Tibet, even today. However, instinct cannot be bred out in a few short generations, and this fact must be recognized from the very outset.

However, with sensible training and an understanding owner, a Tibetan Mastiff can make a most wonderful household companion, but the owner's dedication to the breed is absolutely essential. The Tibetan Mastiff, although often rather stubborn, is quite adaptable. However, he will need human guidance to help him adjust to a lifestyle so far removed from that to which his ancestors were accustomed in Tibet. The Tibetan Mastiff makes a wonderful family dog when mutual respect and understanding between the humans and the dog characterizes this very strong relationship.

The Tibetan Mastiff is a watchdog and has the innate instinct to guard. In Himalayan regions today he is still used for the same purpose, both in the highlands of Tibet and in the homes of the wealthy in cities such as Katmandu in Nepal. The breed's guarding instincts are strong, so they must be kept under control.

The Tibetan Mastiff's primitive nature must be acknowledged. The Tibetan Mastiff will fulfill, by instinct, his centuries-long duties as nighttime sentinel by barking as a warning at everything he hears with his acute hearing. He has a vivid memory, is highly intelligent and is capable of making his own decisions. Therefore he is very independent by nature. A sturdy high fence that cannot be jumped, scaled or dug under is essential for owning this breed, as in addition to being highly independent, the TM is a large and very strong canine who is capable of climbing, digging, jumping and chewing. Some TMs are quite capable of jumping over a 6-foot fence or even higher from a sitting position. The TM may be easily bored and can be very destructive when finding ways to occupy himself.

Many modern-day Tibetan Mastiff owners have noted how fond their dogs are of children. This trait goes back to his ancestors, who were left at home to guard the wife and children while the husband was probably many miles away working on the land. In a domestic situation today, the Tibetan Mastiff makes

Bespeaking the breed's docile yet protective nature, here is Asu Casby, a well-trained Tibetan Mastiff, with Hägar, a four-day-old roebuck.

an extremely loyal family dog, showing both tolerance and patience, especially with children. However, as with any breed, careful adult supervision is essential. In the home, the Tibetan Mastiff is likely to seek out a quiet corner somewhere, where he can keep a watchful eye on everything that is going on around him.

With his owner, the Tibetan Mastiff forms a very close bond and it is easy to consider the dog as another family member. Kept in a family situation, the breed has every opportunity to develop his personality to its full extent and to show his affection and companionship.

When regular visitors are introduced to the home, it is sensible to introduce them carefully, perhaps having the dog on a lead at least for a while. The dog should be praised and encour-

Chewby in the full puppy coat that enables the breed to endure extremes of weather in rough terrain.

LIVESTOCK GUARDIAN
In the US there is increasing interest in using the TM solely as a livestock guardian. However, the TM is best used as a flock and family guardian, as they were used originally in Tibet. The breed's job is that of a sentry, to announce to intruders and predators that their turf and charges are being protected and that they will enforce if necessary.

aged when he has accepted the visitor; this will help him to understand that these people pose no threat.

If a Tibetan Mastiff has his own quarters, perhaps in the yard or in a kennel run, it is only natural that he will protect this area and will threaten anyone who approaches. This must be fully recognized and appreciated about the breed so that owners can style their lives and living spaces accordingly.

Although they are still used as guards in their homeland, no Tibetan Mastiff in the West should be selected purely as a guard. This breed needs companionship and must never be allowed to get bored.

Devotion to the family, property and flock is strong in the breed, so one's Tibetan Mastiff is unlikely to run off to chase animals; instead, he prefers to stay at home with people, animals and things that are familiar to him, all

Owners of the Tibetan Mastiff are deeply devoted to the breed, celebrating its unique temperament and natural beauty.

of which he can protect. It is therefore evident that in the wrong hands a Tibetan Mastiff can be dangerous, for he could harm any intruder, be it human or animal. Yet, brought up and handled correctly, the Tibetan Mastiff can be both stable and reliable.

The Tibetan Mastiff's intelligence can present some problems in both training and showing, for this is a breed of dog with a "thinking brain." It is essential for the trainer to gain the dog's respect; once this has been achieved, the task is undoubtedly easier. Training is necessary for such a large dog, and initially the Tibetan Mastiff is likely to take well to basic obedience training. However, once the tasks become repetitive, he often loses interest. Although he remembers what he has been taught, he can be rather reluctant to obey. Pushing a Tibetan Mastiff into doing something it does not want to do simply will not work.

Tibetan Mastiffs in Switzerland, where the breed fits right into the snowy picturesque environment. Photographer Sanne Rutloh titled this image "Morning Meditation in the Snow."

BARK

The Tibetan Mastiff has a deep, sonorous bark, so charmingly described as being like a well-made copper gong. What better description could there be? However, most gongs are not sounded during the night hours, but the Tibetan Mastiff seems somewhat prone to bellowing at night, especially if left outside. This doubtless goes back again to his ancestors who were set free to prowl at night, warding off any possible intruders.

This, however, should be borne in mind by those living in an urban environment as, however melodious it might sound to our ears, not everyone appreciates the sound of dogs barking at night. Clearly, training can overcome this to a large extent; this is another reason why sensible management of a Tibetan Mastiff is of the utmost importance.

PHYSICAL CHARACTERISTICS

The Tibetan Mastiff is a powerful, heavy and well-built dog with good

Strider demonstrates the solid bone and power that the breed ideally possesses.

LEFT: With the dignity and regal bearing of the breed, Hardin Valley's Tarzan surveys his kingdom. RIGHT: Primitive and elegant, the Tibetan Mastiff sounds the warning bark.

bone. The impression it gives is one of solemnity, but with a kindly appearance. The skull and muzzle are broad, as is the nose with its wide-open nostrils, which are essential for such a substantial breed to survive well in the rarefied air of Tibet. Nothing about the Tibetan Mastiff should look weak. This is an impressive breed with a strong arched neck that is

CONTROL
All Tibetan Mastiffs, whatever their age, should have defined territorial boundaries and a clear understanding that their human owners will always be alpha. TM puppies grow large so quickly that they must be taught manners and respect for pack order from an early age.

Nala (LEFT) and Pabu (RIGHT), both young adult females, show the size and type variations that are found in the breed.

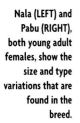

shrouded by a thick mane.

The chest needs to be sufficiently deep and the rib cage capacious enough to allow plenty of room for heart and lungs, which are again essential factors of this breed's make-up because of the environment in which it lived.

The body is a little longer than the dog is high when measured to the top of the shoulder, and its hindquarters should be both powerful and muscular. The cat-shaped feet have good feathering

This modern painting of a Tibetan Mastiff in a nomadic settlement was rendered by one of the author's Tibetan friends.

between the toes, which is something else of great importance to a breed that often had to walk on snow. It is not unusual to find some Tibetan Mastiffs with strong webbing between their toes, another useful asset when living and working on snow-covered ground.

Despite its size, the Tibetan Mastiff is a nimble dog, as was clearly demonstrated at a recent seminar on Tibetan breeds. Some of the TMs there took an interested audience quite by surprise when they negotiated jumps, went through weaving poles and even jumped through tires!

Size

The AKC breed standard specifies that bitches should be a minimum of 24 inches (61 cms) and dogs a minimum of 26 inches (66 cms) in height. It is important to keep in mind that these heights, measured to the top of the shoulder, are at the lowest end of the scale. Tibetan Mastiffs can be much taller than this. Although no weight is specified in the breed standard, this is a heavy dog with good bone.

Evie is a classic Tibetan Mastiff bitch with the white star on her chest, dense coat and mane, and a correct high-set, well-feathered tail.

Ginger displays the rare chocolate brown color described in the AKC standard.

COAT AND COLORS

Even to the casual observer, the coats on Tibetan Mastiffs do seem to differ quite considerably. Firstly, males generally carry heavier coats than their female counterparts, but this is a breed that molts seriously and tends only to be in really full coat during the cooler months of the year.

In general the topcoat is fairly long; beneath this is a heavy and rather woolly undercoat, though this becomes rather sparse when the weather is warm. The coat is a highly practical one when the breed is living at high altitude. It must never be silky or curly; instead it is hard and straight, and stands off from the body, though is definitely not so obviously "stand-off" as the coat of a Chow Chow.

The dense coat on the neck and shoulders gives a mane-like appearance, but this also has a practical function. In its natural habitat, this density of coat serves as admirable protection from the attack of large predators.

Colors permitted in the breed are various, ranging through various shades of gold through to a rich black. Those with tan markings above the eyes, a color combination that can occur in blacks, grays and blues, are called "four eyes." Dogs with four "eyes" are highly prized by the Tibetans, who believe that they have the ability to detect evil in advance.

A white star on the chest is often seen on the Tibetan Mastiff, but this should never be too large. A white star marking symbolizes to Tibetans that the dog has a brave heart. A small amount of white on the feet is also permissible according to the standard, but these markings should never be found elsewhere.

Tibetan Mastiffs rarely need to be bathed, for bathing the coat removes the hair's natural oils. Clearly the occasional bath can do

GOOD CHEWERS

Tibetan Mastiffs, especially if bored, are highly adept at being escape artists. Unfortunately for their owners, many thoroughly enjoy chewing wood, and they can be quite determined. Apparently, one Tibetan Mastiff chewed his way through the front door and was found in the yard when his owners returned home.

no harm, and may indeed be necessary if the coat has for some reason become particularly dirty or if it needs tidying up for a show.

TAIL
The high-set tail is well feathered, though more sparsely so when in molt, and is curled over the back to one side. This tail carriage is very characteristic of Tibetan breeds of dog.

HEALTH CONSIDERATIONS
The Tibetan Mastiff evolved in an area with difficult living conditions, so it was certainly a case of only the fittest surviving long enough to reproduce their kind. As a result, the breed is in general a hardy one, and for its size the breed is reasonably long-lived. All dogs, whatever their breed, can suffer health problems occasionally, but thankfully the Tibetan Mastiff has few inherited problems.

ENTROPION
Entropion is a problem that has been known to occur occasionally in the breed, though most breeders have organized their breeding programs so as not to use affected animals. This condition involves the eyelids turning inward so that the eyelashes press against the cornea. Corrective surgery is usually possible, but both dogs and bitches that are so affected should certainly not be used in breeding programs.

CANINE INHERITED DEMYELINATIVE NEUROPATHY (CIDN)
Going back to the late 1970s, some Tibetan Mastiff puppies suffered from a condition that affected the peripheral nervous system. Original diagnosis was incorrect, for it was thought to have been due to injury of the pelvis. However, much important work was carried out, and the condition, now correctly named canine inherited demyelinative neuropathy and first detected and diagnosed by researchers at Cornell University, is known to involve the nerve fibers. These nerve fibers cannot transmit impulses from the spinal cord to the muscles due to degeneration of the myelin sheath surrounding them.

Puppies appear normal at birth, but by about six weeks of age they lose muscle tone in their hindquarters, which become weak. This becomes worse, usually over a period of two to five weeks;

"Look into my eyes." With his dark eyes and soulful expression, the Tibetan Mastiff has a face that's hard to forget.

puppies that are severely affected cannot walk, sometimes being unable even to stand. The condition gradually progresses to complete paralysis of the rear quarters. There is no treatment available.

The researchers at Cornell discovered that a simple autosomal recessive gene was the mode of transmission. The number of Tibetan Mastiffs carrying this gene is limited; moreover, dedicated breeders have been honest enough to take great care in their breeding programs. Twenty-five years of breeders' cooperation in conjunction with researchers' findings have drastically reduced the probability that any Tibetan Mastiff puppy will be born with this condition.

HIP AND ELBOW DYSPLASIA

Hip dysplasia occurs in many breeds, particularly in the larger, heavier breeds. It is a problem involving the malformation of the ball and socket joint at the hip; this joint must have a very tight fit or else the ball will dislocate and cause pain, eventually arthritis. The first sign, a "bunny-hopping" gait or limp, usually appears around four to nine months of age.

Hip dysplasia is thought to be a result of both genetic and environmental factors. Rapid growth and weight gain have been linked to the condition. As preventive measures, do not allow your puppy to become overweight and do not supplement his diet with calcium unless directed by your veterinarian. Puppy food should be formulated for large-breed puppies and contain less than 1.2% calcium.

For affected dogs, there are both surgical and medical treatment options. Conscientious breeders routinely x-ray their breeding stock, have the x-rays evaluated and graded by the Orthopedic Foundation of America (OFA) and breed only animals with sound hips. Ask your breeder what policies they follow.

Another similar condition that can affect the Tibetan Mastiff is elbow dysplasia, in which the elbow joint is not formed correctly, possibly due to different growth rates of three bones found in the joint. For affected dogs, surgical options as well as medical management with anti-inflammatory drugs are available.

Like hip dysplasia, elbow dysplasia is an inherited condition that also is influenced by environment. Follow the same guidelines for diet and weight control as with hip dysplasia. The Orthopedic Foundation of America also has an x-ray screening and rating program for elbows, so ask your breeder about his testing policies for elbow dysplasia.

SEASONAL CYCLES
Traditionally, in Tibet, TM bitches only cycled once a year, with puppies born during winter months. Now, removed from the climate extremes of Tibet, Western TM bitches may cycle every 6-9 months, a result of warmer climate and better nutrition.

AUTOIMMUNE HYPOTHYROIDISM
This is the most common endocrine condition found in large-breed dogs, and the Tibetan Mastiff is no exception. Signs to look for are mental dullness manifested as decreased energy level and less interest in play and activities, increase in sleeping, weight gain, poor skin and coat condition (e.g., flaking, scaling) and recurrent ear infections.

Once diagnosed, this condition can be treated very effectively and quite affordably with daily thyroid supplementation. Although the mode of inheritance is not known, hypothyroidism is thought to have a genetic component because of the familial nature of the breed. Breeders should screen their breeding stock and avoid breeding affected dogs.

OSTEOCHONDRITIS DISSECANS
This condition, also called OCD, is the result of an underlying bone defect where the cartilage lifts off the bone and creates a flap. The cartilage becomes thickened and cracked, causes inflammation and pain and can eventually lead to degeneration of the joint. The most frequently diagnosed site is the shoulder but the elbow, hock and stifle may also be affected. Bilateral joints are often involved and male dogs are affected more frequently than females.

This condition may have both hereditary and environmental factors. As a preventive, keep your puppy lean, and do not give calcium supplements or over-exercise him. Left untreated, the prognosis is variable. Surgical treatment is often recommended. As OCD has a hereditary component, affected dogs should not be bred.

PANOSTEITIS
Sometimes also referred to as "growing pains," panosteitis is an inflammation of the long bones that occurs in young large-breed dogs. Lameness will appear suddenly, without reason, and shift from leg to leg. The disease itself is self-limiting and resolves on its own over time. Pain medication can be prescribed during times of lameness.

Special thanks to health and genetics chairperson Corinne Foster of the Tibetan Mastiff Club of America for information on health concerns in the breed.

No one said owning a TM was easy (hopefully)! Your TM is looking to you to be the loving and caring owner you promised to be when you first acquired him, not just for one year or two years, but for the rest of his life. The TM can be an extraordinary pet, but establishing that relationship takes time, patience and, yes, money.

The Tibetan Mastiff is a "guardian" breed and not a guard dog. If you are looking for a guard dog, one that can be trained to attack someone on command, you are not looking for a Tibetan Mastiff. Training Tibetan Mastiffs for guard-dog work has proven to be unsuccessful. The Tibetan Mastiff was never meant to attack, but rather to scare off and intimidate as a guardian...not to bite. The Tibetan Mastiff has an uncanny way of determining who or what is a threat to his territory and/or owner. That instinct can't be trained into the dog.

If you just can't handle destruction to your home, yard, car, shoes etc., or if you don't have the time or patience for training and understanding your Tibetan Mastiff, then the Tibetan Mastiff is not for you!

FACTS:

- The Tibetan Mastiff is a slow-maturing breed in which the "puppyhood" stage can last for years, not months. Do you have the fortitude to last that long with modifying your home, yard, etc., to suit your TM?
- The Tibetan Mastiff is very attached to his owners. Are you prepared to spend time with your Tibetan Mastiff for his lifetime (15 years or more, quite possibly). If not, are you prepared for an active TM that can be very destructive in your home?
- The Tibetan Mastiff is a guardian breed who thinks independently and works instead of people, not with people. Are you prepared to respect and deal with this appropriately?
- The main reasons that people relinquish their Tibetan Mastiffs to rescue are:
  1. Destructive behavior
  2. Excessive barking
  3. Escaping
  4. Dominance over other animals
  5. Overprotectiveness with family

If you are not prepared to deal with the worst possible scenarios and are not prepared for the surprises that many TMs may throw your way, then the TM is not for you!

Rescue organizations should not be your first line of defense when you and your TM have issues. You should first contact the person you got your TM from for honest advice on how to help you deal with your difficulties (assuming you got your dog from a breeder). Follow the breeder's advice! If that doesn't help, contact the breeder again to discuss the problem(s).

Remember, you have a Tibetan Mastiff that will act like, think like and always be a Tibetan Mastiff, unlike any other breed you may have or have had. Your TM may also act much differently than someone else's Tibetan Mastiff, and that's to be expected as they are all individuals (just like humans) and need to be dealt with as individuals. If need be, a professional trainer who specializes in behavioral issues may be in order.

The people who help out in rescues and with rehoming (breed clubs, rescue groups, enthusiasts, breeders, owners) are angels, but not miracle workers. They can't possibly take in and/or cover the costs of every dog. Rescue is a huge job, and the people involved devote their emotional energy, time (often very long and irregular hours), money (for crates, transportation costs, vet bills, housing, phone bills, food, etc.), knowledge and more, all on someone else's TM. Rescue organizations should be contacted if there is a legitimate reason for someone's giving up his dog, only after all other avenues have been taken.

Lastly, the relationship between you and your TM should be mutual. Tibetan Mastiffs have the most wonderful, almost magical, spirits. The TM spirit is sensitive and easily broken, which results in an angry or depressed state that will be easy to recognize in your TM. When the relationship is mutual, the bond between you and your dog will flourish into everything it should be: a very happy owner and a very happy Tibetan Mastiff.

REASONS FOR GIVING UP A DOG THAT ARE NOT LEGITIMATE INCLUDE:

- "We have a baby on the way." In this case, you should be getting information on how to introduce the new baby into the family unit (which includes your TM!) and how to introduce the dog to your baby.
- "He destroyed the inside of the car." Common sense would tell you that the dog should be crated or confined behind a safety gate when in the car.
- "He jumped the fence again." Get a higher fence!

PUPPY-BUYER CHECKLIST
From information provided by the Tibetan Mastiff Club of America

QUESTIONS TO ASK YOURSELF

1. Do I have enough time for a dog?
2. Do I have adequate space and housing?
3. Can I afford complete veterinary care and am I prepared to find a good veterinarian who is experienced with large-breed dogs?
4. Am I prepared to feed a high-quality diet and do I understand the dietary needs of a large-breed dog?
5. Am I willing to be patient with house-training?
6. Am I willing to be patient with obedience training and am I prepared to find an appropriate obedience class?
7. Am I prepared to deal with the highly territorial nature of the adult Tibetan Mastiff?
8. Am I prepared to deal with the Tibetan Mastiff's nocturnal barking?
9. Am I prepared to be the "top dog," the alpha, in my pack?
10. Can I deal with my belongings being chewed or possibly destroyed during the breed's puppyhood, which can last several years? Am I prepared to provide my dog with a lot of safe chew toys?
11. Am I willing to teach my children and ensure that they properly treat, hold, care for and respect their TM as a puppy and as an adult dog? Am I prepared to take responsibility for this dog and his needs, as this is not something that can be left to the children?
12. Am I prepared to keep my breeder informed about the dog's achievements and/or problems?
13. Am I prepared to find suitable care for my dog if I am away on vacation or for business? Am I prepared to find housing that allows animals if I have to move? Will I continue to accept responsibility for my dog in all situations that may occur and any life changes?
14. Am I prepared to make a commitment for the entire lifetime of this dog, which should be upwards of ten years?

QUESTIONS TO ASK YOUR BREEDER

1. Are you knowledgeable about the breed? How many years have you been breeding? To what organizations do you belong and in what competitive events are you involved with your dogs?
2. Will you be available to answer questions and give advice for the lifetime of this dog?
3. Do you give a guarantee against health and temperament problems?
4. Are the pup's sire and dam at least two years of age?
5. Do the sire and dam both have their hip and elbow clearances from the OFA or PennHIP (a vet's "OK" is not sufficient)? What about the pup's grandparents, siblings of the parents and other puppies that these parents have produced?
6. Can I meet the parents? Can you tell me about their temperament and health, as well as that of other relatives? Have any relatives died at a young age and why?
7. Have the parents produced any puppies with serious health problems?
8. Have the pups been raised in the home? Do they look and seem healthy; are their coats full and clean; and are they active and energetic?
9. Have the pups had their first shots, wormings and temperament tests?
10. Will you provide a pedigree from a recognized registry, the pup's health records and information on feeding, training and care?
11. Will you be willing to help rehome the dog if the need arises in the future and will you take the dog back if a suitable new home cannot be found?

TIBETAN MASTIFF

Multi-Ch. Strazce z Tibetu Mimayin. This is what the FCI standard means when it states: "The impressive head provides a noble and dignified look, enhanced by a mane around the head and neck."

All breed standards are designed effectively to paint a picture in words, though each reader will almost certainly have a slightly different way of interpreting these words. However, to fully comprehend the intricacies of a breed, reading words alone is never enough; it is essential also for devotees to watch the Tibetan Mastiffs being judged at shows and, if possible, to attend seminars at which the breed is discussed. This enables owners to absorb as much as possible about the breed they love so much.

The standard conveys immediately that a typical Tibetan Mastiff is powerful, heavy, well built and with good bone. Hence, it takes little comprehension to realize immediately that a Tibetan Mastiff of finely built construction, with little substance or power, would be thoroughly untypical of the breed.

Further, most judges, I find, pay little or no attention to the movement of the breed when walking, although it is clear in the standard that, when walking, the Tibetan Mastiff should appear slow and very deliberate. How can a judge determine this if he or she only views the breed when moving quickly?

A breed standard undoubtedly helps breeders to breed stock that comes as close as possible to the recognized standard, and helps judges to know exactly what they are looking for. The standard enables a judge to make a carefully considered decision when selecting the most typical Tibetan Mastiff present to head his or her line of winners.

THE AMERICAN KENNEL CLUB BREED STANDARD FOR THE TIBETAN MASTIFF

General Appearance: Powerful, heavy, well built dog, well muscled, with much substance and bone, and of solemn but kindly appearance. The Tibetan Mastiff stands well up on the pasterns, with strong, tight, cat feet, giving an alert appearance. The body is slightly longer than tall. The head is broad and impressive, with massive back skull, the eyes deep-set and almond shaped, slightly slanted, the muzzle broad and well-padded, giving a square appearance. The typical expression of the breed is one of watchfulness. The tail is well feathered and carried over the back in a single curl falling over the loin, balancing the head. The coat and heavy mane is thick, with coarse guard hair and a wooly undercoat. The tail and britches are well feathered.

The Tibetan Mastiff has been used primarily as a family and property guardian for many millennia, and is aloof and watchful of strangers, and highly protective of its people and property.

Size, Proportion, Substance: *Size:* Dogs—minimum of 26 inches at the withers. Bitches—minimum of 24 inches at the withers. Dogs and bitches that are more than one inch below the minimum heights to be severely faulted. *Proportion:* Slightly longer than tall (9–10), (i.e., the height to length, measured from sternum to ischium should be slightly greater than the distance from withers to ground). *Substance:* The Tibetan Mastiff should have impressive substance, both in bone and structure, as well as strength. When dogs are judged equal in type, proportion and movement, the more substantial dog, in terms of substance and bone, not merely height, is to be given preference.

Head: Broad, heavy and strong. Some wrinkling in maturity, extending from above eyes down

World Ch. Drakyi Senge Sundari exemplifies the Tibetan Mastiff's impressive substance in bone, structure, size and strength.

to corner of mouth. A correct head and expression is essential to the breed. *Expression:* Noble, intelligent, watchful and aloof. *Eyes:* Very expressive, medium size, any shade of brown. Rims to be black except in blue/grey, blue/grey and tan dogs and brown dogs, the darkest possible shade of grey or brown. Eyes deep-set, well apart, almond-shaped and slightly slanting. Any other color or shape to be severely faulted since it detracts from the typical expression. *Ears:* Medium size, V-shaped, pendant, set-on high, dropping forward and hanging close to head. Raised when alert, on level with the top of the skull. The ear leather is thick, covered with soft short hair, and when measured, should reach the inner corner of the eye. *Skull:* Broad and large, with strongly defined occiput. Broad back skull. *Stop:* Deep and well defined. *Muzzle:* Broad, well filled and square when viewed from all sides. *Proportions:* Measurement from occiput to stop and stop to end of nose, equal or slightly shorter. *Nose:* Broad, well pigmented, with open nostrils. Black, except with blue/grey or blue/grey and tan dogs, the darkest shade of grey and brown dogs, the darkest shade of brown. Any other color to be severely faulted. *Lips:* Well developed, thick, with moderate flews and slightly pendulous lower lips. *Bite:* Complete scissor bite. Level bite acceptable. Essential that dentition fits tightly, to maintain square form of muzzle. *Teeth:* Canine teeth large, strong, broken teeth not to be faulted. *Faults:* Missing teeth, overshot, undershot bite.

Neck, Topline and Body: *Neck:* The neck is well muscled, moderately arched, and may have moderate dewlap. The neck, especially in dogs, is shrouded by a thick upstanding mane. *Topline:* Topline straight and level between withers and croup. *Body:* The chest is rather deep, of moderate breadth, with reasonable spring of rib. Brisket reaching to just below elbows. Underline with pronounced (but not exaggerated) tuck-up. The back is muscular with firmly muscled loin. There is no slope or angle to the croup. *Tail:* Medium to long, but not reaching below hock joint; well feathered. Set high on line with top of back. When alert or in motion, curled over back or to one side. Tails that are double curled or carried in an incomplete curl to be faulted.

Forequarters: *Shoulders:* Well laid back, muscular, strongly boned, with moderate angulation to match the rear angulation. *Legs:* Straight, with substantial bone and muscle, well covered with short, coarse hair, feathering, and with strong pasterns that have a slight slope. *Feet:* Cat feet. Fairly large, strong, compact, may have feathering between toes. Nails may be either black and/or white, regardless of coat color. A single dewclaw may be present on the front feet.

Hindquarters: *Hindquarters:* Powerful, muscular, with all parts being moderately angulated. Seen from behind, the hind legs and stifle are parallel. The hocks are strong, well let down (approximately one-third the overall length of the leg), and perpendicular. *Feet:* A single or double dewclaw may be present on the rear feet. Removal of rear dewclaws, if present, optional.

Coat: In general, dogs carry noticeably more coat than bitches. The quality of the coat is of greater importance than quantity. Double-coated, with fairly long, thick coarse guard hair, with heavy soft undercoat in cold weather which becomes rather sparse in warmer months. Hair is fine but hard, straight and stand-off; never silky, curly or wavy. Heavy undercoat, when present, rather woolly. Neck and shoulders heavily coated, especially in dogs, giving mane-like appearance. Tail and britches densely coated and heavily feathered. The Tibetan Mastiff is

shown naturally. Trimming is not acceptable except to provide a clean cut appearance of feet. Dogs are not to be penalized if shown with a summer coat.

Color: Black, brown and blue/grey, all with or without tan markings, and various shades of gold. Tan ranges from a very rich shade through a lighter color. White markings on breast and feet acceptable. Tan markings may appear at any or all of the following areas: above eyes as spots, around eyes (including spectacle markings), on each side of the muzzle, on throat, on lower part of front forelegs and extending up the inside of the forelegs, on inside of rear legs showing down the front of the

Head study showing pleasing type, proper structure and correct substance.

Mature, substantial dog in profile showing correct type, balance and structure.

stifle and broadening out to the front of the rear legs from hock to toes, on breeches, and underside of tail. Undercoat, as well as furnishings on breeches and underside of tail, may be lighter shades of the dominant color. The undercoat on black and tan dogs also may be grey or tan. Other markings such as sabling, brindling, white on other areas of the body, or large white markings, to be faulted. All other coat colors, while accepted, are to be faulted.

Gait: The gait of a Tibetan Mastiff is powerful, steady and balanced, yet at the same time, light-footed. When viewed from the side, reach and drive should indicate maximum use of the dog's moderate angulation. Back remains level and firm. Sound and powerful movement more important than speed.

Temperament: The Tibetan Mastiff is a highly intelligent, independent, strong willed and rather reserved dog. He is aloof with strangers and highly protective of his charges and his property. In the ring he may exhibit reserve or lack of enthusiasm, but any sign of shyness is unacceptable and must be severely faulted as inappropriate for a guardian breed. Conversely, given its aloof nature, judges should also beware of putting a premium on showiness.

Approved: November 8, 2004
Effective: January 1, 2005
© 2005 American Tibetan
Mastiff Association

THE UKC BREED STANDARD FOR THE TIBETAN MASTIFF

History: The Tibetan Mastiff, or Do-Khyi, is a large working dog from the Himalayas. Tracing the breed's history back to antiquity, it acted as the guardian and companion of the Tibetan villagers and nomads, as well as being the traditional guardian of the Tibetan monasteries. Documented accounts by Marco Polo, who went to Asia in 1271, praise the breed's natural strength and physical and mental impressiveness. Even its deep bark has been described as a unique and highly treasured feature of the breed. Many cynologists consider the Tibetan Mastiff the forefather of all large mountain and mastiff breeds.

The Tibetan Mastiff was recognized by the United Kennel Club in 1998.

General Appearance and Characteristics: Large, sound and powerfully built. Well-boned and muscled, never light or refined; always agile. The impressive head provides a noble and dignified look, enhanced by a mane around the head and neck. The head is balanced by a curled tail carried over the back. Males are larger than the females, with heavier features and carrying more coat. The Tibetan Mastiff is still widely used in its traditional role as a natural guardian of family and flock, and has an aloof and independent nature.

A loyal companion and natural guardian. Highly intelligent, strong-willed, independent, aloof and protective when necessary. Patient and tolerant; may be wary of strangers. Any reserve, protectiveness or lack of enthusiasm when exhibited should not be penalized provided the dog can be properly evaluated.

Head and Skull: The head is broad, heavy and strong. The skull is massive, with a strongly defined occiput and marked stop. Proportions from occiput to stop, and stop to the end of the nose, range from equal lengths (1 to 1), to a muzzle that is somewhat shorter than the length of the topskull (2 to 3). *Muzzle*—Fairly broad, well padded, blunt and square when viewed from all sides. Broad nose, well-opened nostrils. Lips well-developed, with moderate flews. Some wrinkling, with maturity, on the head extending from above the

FAULTS IN PROFILE

Lacking bone and substance, upright shoulders, narrow front, toes out in front, high in the rear, narrow and lacking angulation behind.

Generally lacking substance throughout, ewe-necked, upright shoulders, soft topline, low tailset, weak rear, very straight behind.

Significant lack of angulation front and rear, heavy shoulders, weak underdeveloped rear, roached back.

Excessive dewlap, long-backed, low on leg, toes out in front, dip behind withers, steep in croup, low tailset, cow-hocked.

eyes to the corner of the mouth. Hair is short on the face developing into a distinct mane, from the crown to the withers, surrounding the head and neck. *Eyes*—Very expressive, medium size; various shades of brown color preferred, other colors acceptable. More sunken than prominent, set well apart, oval, and slightly slanting. A slight haw may be present. *Ears*—Medium size to somewhat larger, triangular, pendent, carried rather high, hanging close to the head when in repose. When at attention, level with the top of skull and brought forward, appearing to broaden the skull. Ear leathers covered with soft short hair. *Teeth*—Full dentition fitting tightly to maintain strong chin. Jaws and teeth strong with regular scissors bite, set square to the jaw. Level bite acceptable. Overshot and undershot bites, missing teeth are to be faulted to the degree present. Broken teeth are not to be faulted.

Neck: The neck is strong, arched and well muscled. There may be some dewlap.

Forequarters: Well laid shoulders, muscular and strongly boned. Straight legs with strong, slightly sloping pasterns.

Body: Topline is level with straight back. *Body*—The chest is rather deep and of moderate breadth.

Broad muscular loins, very slightly sloping croup. Ribs are well-sprung, not barreled. Brisket reaching to or just below the elbows.

Hindquarters: Powerful, muscular with moderate angulation and strong lower-set hocks. Hind legs seen from behind are parallel.

Feet: The feet are fairly large, strong, with thick pads, rounded and compact. There may be some feathering between the toes.

Tail: The tail is medium to long, well feathered, set high and carried over the back. A tail with a single curl is preferred, but other configurations are acceptable.

Coat: Double coated. Long, coarse guard hairs with a heavy, wooly undercoat that becomes sparse in warmer months and warmer climates. Quality and correctness of coat is of greater importance than quantity. Hair hard and straight, slight wave at the topline, never curly. Neck and shoulders heavily coated, giving a mane-like appearance that is more pronounced in mature males. Tail and upper rear parts of hind legs well feathered. The Tibetan Mastiff is exhibited in a natural condition with no trimming. Seasonal shedding is not to be penalized.

Color: Black, chocolate brown and slate gray, all with or without tan markings, as well as various shades of gold. The shades of gold and the tan markings may range from cream to dark red/gold, with or without sable/black tipping. White markings may occur on chest, neck and feet.

Pigmentation on lips, nose and eye rims is black, except on dilute colors (chocolate, blue and gold dilute) where the pigmentation is also diluted.

Height and Weight: *Size*—Dogs: minimum 26 inches (ranging to over 30 inches). Bitches: minimum 24 inches (ranging to over 28 inches). Though appearing square, the body is slightly longer than high (10 to 9), front and rear angulation is balanced. Slow to mature, dogs range from 100 to 160+ pounds. Bitches range from 75 to 120+ pounds. Preference is given to dogs of greater height, provided that their proportions are harmonious, and that proper type, substance, structure and breed characteristics are present.

Gait: Powerful; moves with purpose and agility, and is capable of considerable speed. Measured and deliberate when walking. At speed will tend toward, and may reach, a single track.

Disqualifications: Unilateral or bilateral cryptorchid. Viciousness or extreme shyness. Albinism.

TIBETAN MASTIFF

WHERE TO BEGIN?

Before deciding to look for a puppy, it is essential that you are fully clear in your mind that the Tibetan Mastiff is the right breed for you and your family. You should have done plenty of research on the breed, for the Tibetan Mastiff in the wrong hands will certainly not make an easy pet. No dog should be moved from one home to another because his owners were thoughtless enough not to have considered the implications of taking on such a breed.

If you are convinced that the Tibetan Mastiff is the ideal dog for you, it's time to learn about where to find a puppy and what to look for. You should contact the national breed clubs to find breeders in your area who enjoy a good reputation in the breed. You are looking for a breeder with outstanding dog ethics and a strong commitment to the breed. New owners should have many questions, and a dedicated breeder is indeed the one to answer your questions and make you comfortable with your choice of the Tibetan Mastiff. Likewise, a good breeder will sell you a puppy at a fair price if, and only if, the breeder determines that you are a suitable, worthy owner of his dogs. An established breeder

SELECTING FROM THE LITTER

Before you visit a litter of puppies, promise yourself that you won't fall for the first pretty face you see! Decide on your goals for your puppy—show/breeding prospect, obedience competitor, family companion—and then look for a puppy who displays the appropriate qualities. In most litters, there is an alpha pup (the bossy puppy), and occasionally a shy fellow who is less confident, with the rest of the litter falling somewhere in the middle. "Middle-of-the-roaders" are safe bets for most families and novice competitors.

can be relied upon for advice for the lifetime of your dog. A reputable breeder will accept a puppy or adult dog back should you no longer be able to care for the dog. When choosing a breeder, reputation is much more important than convenience of location. With a rare breed like the TM, you are not likely to find a breeder nearby. Fortunately, most Tibetan Mastiff breeders are devoted to the breed and its well-being.

The American Tibetan Mastiff Association (www.tibetanmastiff.org), which is the breed's AKC parent club, and the Tibetan Mastiff Club of America (www.tmcamerica.org), which is affiliated with the United Kennel Club, are two trusted sources for breeder referrals in the US; there are also some reputable TM breeders in Canada. Potential owners are also encouraged to attend dog shows to see the Tibetan Mastiffs in action, to meet the owners and handlers firsthand and to get an idea of what Tibetan Mastiffs look

"Who is that good-looking creature?"

like outside a photographer's lens. Provided you approach the handlers after they have finished showing, most are more than willing to answer questions, recommend breeders and give advice.

Tibetan Mastiff puppies invariably look enchanting, but you must select one from a caring breeder who has given the puppies all the attention they deserve and has looked after them well. It would be wise to check with the Tibetan Mastiff breed club of which your breeder is a member to see what health testing they require and to be sure to see documentation of these tests on the litter's parents (and pups if applicable).

Once you have contacted and met a breeder or two and made

SIGNS OF A HEALTHY PUPPY

Healthy puppies are robust, alert and active, sporting shiny coats and supple skin. They should not appear lethargic, bloated or pot-bellied, nor should they have flaky skin or runny or crusted eyes or noses. Their stools should be firm and well formed, with no evidence of blood or mucus.

Although it's easy to fall in love with every TM pup you meet, use your head and take the breeder's recommendations into account when choosing a pup. This nine-week-old litter is from the Hardin Valley kennel.

your choice about which breeder is best suited to your needs, it's time to visit the litter. Keep in mind that many top breeders have waiting lists. Sometimes new owners have to wait a year or more for a puppy. If you are really committed to the breeder whom

A slightly damp but completely adorable female gold sable puppy.

you've selected, then you will wait (and hope for an early arrival!). If not, you may have to go with another reputable breeder.

The size of a Tibetan Mastiff litter varies, but on the average is between six and eight pups. However, litters of Tibetan Mastiffs are few and far between. Therefore, if you have a personal color preference, you may have no choice as to color, although puppies of varying colors can be born within one litter. Sex of your puppy is another thing to consider—do you want a male or a female? In the Tibetan Mastiff, the males are larger than females and noticeably carry more coat. Whatever your preferences regarding coat color and sex, you should always be certain that the puppy you finally select has a sound personality. Do not take pity on an unduly shy puppy, for in doing so you will be asking for trouble in the long term. Such a pup is likely to have serious problems becoming socialized.

Keep in mind that a young puppy will look quite different from an adult. The puppy coat looks almost like the fluff one might find on a teddy bear; only with maturity will this develop into the thick double coat so characteristic of the adult TM. A Tibetan Mastiff will reach its full height during puppyhood, but continues to develop physically for much longer. Bitches reach their best between two and three years of age, and dogs not until at least four years old.

Breeders commonly allow visitors to see the litter by around the fifth or sixth week, and puppies leave for their new homes between the eighth and

Spreading the Christmas spirit can wear a puppy out!

tenth week. Breeders who permit their puppies to leave early are more interested in your money than their puppies' well being.

Puppies need to learn the rules of the pack from their dams, and most dams continue teaching the pups manners and dos and don'ts until around the eighth week. Breeders spend significant amounts of time with the Tibetan Mastiff toddlers so that they are able to interact with the "other species," i.e., humans. Given the long history that dogs and humans have, bonding between the two species is natural but must be nurtured.

A Tibetan Mastiff puppy should look well fed, but not pot-bellied, as this might indicate worms. The eyes should look bright and clear, without discharge, and gums should be pink, not nearly white. There should be no discharge from the

PUPPY SELECTION

Your selection of a good puppy can be determined by your needs. A show potential or a good pet? It is your choice. Every puppy, however, should be of good temperament. Although show-quality puppies are bred and raised with emphasis on physical conformation, responsible breeders strive for equally good temperament. Do not buy from a breeder who concentrates solely on physical beauty at the expense of personality.

COST OF OWNERSHIP

The purchase price of your puppy is merely the first expense in the typical dog budget. Quality dog food, veterinary care (sickness and health maintenance), dog supplies and grooming costs will add up to big bucks every year. Can you adequately afford to support a canine addition to the family?

nose, and certainly no evidence of loose stools. The puppy you choose should have a healthy-looking coat with absolutely no sign of parasites. Also check the bite of your selected puppy to be sure that it is neither overshot nor undershot; a scissors bite is preferred, although a level bite is acceptable.

A COMMITTED NEW OWNER

By now you should understand what makes the Tibetan Mastiff a most unique and special breed, one that is not the breed for everyone and is best for experienced owners. If you have researched breeders, you should be able to recognize a knowledgeable and responsible Tibetan Mastiff breeder who cares not only about his pups but also about the best interest of the breed and what kind of owner you will be. If you have completed the next step in your exciting journey, you have found a litter of quality Tibetan Mastiff pups.

A visit with the puppies and their breeder should be an education in itself. Breed research, breeder selection and puppy visitation are essential aspects of finding the puppy of your dreams. Beyond that, these things also lay the foundation for a successful future with your pup. Puppy personalities within each litter vary, from the shy and easygoing puppy to the one who is dominant and assertive, with most pups falling somewhere in between. By spending time with the puppies, you will be able to recognize certain behaviors and what these behaviors indicate about each pup's temperament. Which type of pup will complement your family dynamics is best determined by observing the puppies in action within their "pack." Your breeder's expertise and recommendations are so valuable. Although you may fall

Newborn TM pups resting on mom's front paw. Can you believe that TMs start out this small?

in love with a bold and brassy male, the breeder may suggest that another pup would be best for you. The breeder's experience in rearing Tibetan Mastiff pups and matching their temperaments with appropriate humans offers the best assurance that your pup will meet your needs and expectations. The type of puppy that you select is just as important as your decision that the Tibetan Mastiff is the breed for you.

The decision to live with a Tibetan Mastiff is a serious commitment and not one to be taken lightly. This puppy is a living sentient being that will be dependent on you for basic survival for his entire life. Beyond the basics of survival—food, water, shelter and protection—he needs much, much more. The new pup needs love, nurturing and a proper canine education to mold him into a responsible, well-behaved canine citizen. The trials

Two five-and-a-half-week-old pups from Everest North's "Auspicious" litter: Bruno on the left and Thor on the right.

of puppyhood, including chewing and potential damage to property, can last several years. Your Tibetan Mastiff's health and good manners will need consistent monitoring and regular "tune-ups," so your job as a responsible dog owner will be ongoing throughout every stage of his life. If you are not prepared to accept these responsibilities and commit to them for the dog's entire lifetime, then you are not prepared to own a dog of any breed.

Although the responsibilities of owning a dog may at times tax your patience, the joy of living with your Tibetan Mastiff far outweighs the workload, and a well-mannered adult dog is worth your time and effort. Before your very eyes, your new charge will grow up to be your most loyal friend, devoted to you unconditionally.

NEW RELEASES

Most breeders release their puppies between eight and ten weeks of age. The seventh week is crucial for social interaction between TM littermates, and puppies should never be sent to new homes before then. This also allows for an additional vaccination and more acquired immune protection. Trust a breeder's recommendation for the puppy that best suits your family. Breeders should know their stock.

GETTING ACQUAINTED

When visiting a litter, ask the breeder for suggestions on how best to interact with the puppies. If possible, get right into the middle of the pack and sit down with them. Observe which pups climb into your lap and which ones shy away. Toss a toy for them to chase and bring back to you. It's easy to fall in love with the first puppy who picks you, but take your breeder's advice and think it over carefully before your make your final decision.

YOUR TM SHOPPING LIST

Just as expectant parents prepare a nursery for their baby, so should you ready your home for the arrival of your Tibetan Mastiff pup. If you have the necessary puppy supplies purchased and in place before he comes home, it will ease the puppy's transition from the warmth and familiarity of his mom and littermates to the brand-new environment of his new home and human family. You will be too busy to stock up and prepare your house after your pup comes home, that's for sure! Imagine how a pup must feel upon being transported to a strange new place. It's up to you to comfort him and to let your little pup know that he is going to be happy with you.

FOOD AND WATER BOWLS

Your puppy will need separate bowls for his food and water. Stainless steel pans are generally preferred over plastic bowls since they sterilize better and pups are less inclined to chew on the metal. Heavy-duty ceramic bowls are popular, but consider how often you will have to pick up those heavy bowls. Buy adult-sized pans, as your puppy will grow into them before you know it. For the Tibetan Mastiff's drinking water, an extra-large water-cooler-style system is recommended, in which water jugs continously supply fresh, clean water.

THE DOG CRATE

While the use of crates with dogs in general is on the rise, adult Tibetan Mastiffs usually are not crated except for travel purposes. The crate, however, can be a very helpful tool for puppy house-breaking, safety and preventing destructive behavior.

most popular. Both are safe and your puppy will adjust to either one, so the choice is up to you. The wire crates offer better visibility for the pup as well as better ventilation. Many of the wire crates easily collapse into suitcase-size carriers. The fiberglass crates, similar to those used by the airlines for animal transport, are sturdier and more den-like. However, the fiberglass crates do not collapse and are less ventilated than a wire crate, which can be problematic in hot weather. Some of the newer crates are made of heavy plastic mesh; they are very lightweight and fold up into slim-line suitcases. However, a mesh crate might not be suitable for a pup with manic chewing habits.

Don't bother with a puppy-sized crate. Although your Tibetan Mastiff will be a wee fellow when you bring him home, he will grow up in the blink of an eye and your

Your local pet shop usually has a wide variety of crates, but the Tibetan Mastiff needs a very large crate and it might have to be ordered for you.

Because dogs are natural den creatures that prefer cave-like environments, the benefits of crate use are many. The crate provides the puppy with his very own "safe house," a cozy place to sleep, take a break or seek comfort with a favorite toy; a travel aid to house your dog when on the road, at motels or at the vet's office; a training aid to help teach your puppy proper toileting habits; and a place of solitude when non-dog people happen to drop by and don't want a lively puppy—or even a well-behaved adult dog—saying hello or begging for attention. If your TM is accustomed to a crate as a pup, he will accept it as an adult when the need for crating arises.

Crates come in several types, although the wire crate and the fiberglass airline-type crate are the

Cuteness and dignity combined—even young pups have the regal look so typical of the breed.

Osa is a black and tan puppy with the white star/blaze on his chest that in Tibet signifies a brave heart.

CRATE EXPECTATIONS

To make the crate more inviting to your puppy, you can offer his first meal or two inside the crate, always keeping the crate door open so that he does not feel confined. Keep a favorite toy or two in the crate for him to play with while inside. You can also cover the crate at night with a lightweight sheet to make it more den-like and remove the stimuli of household activity. Never put him into his crate as punishment or as you are scolding him, since he will then associate his crate with negative situations and avoid going there. Crates should never be used to confine pups in lieu of a spacious kennel run or safely enclosed yard.

TOYS 'R SAFE

The vast array of tantalizing puppy toys is staggering. Stroll through any pet shop or pet-supply outlet and you will see that the choices can be overwhelming. However, not all dog toys are safe or sensible. Most very young puppies enjoy soft woolly toys, but TM pups usually destroy and ingest them, which can be dangerous. Further, avoid toys that have buttons, tabs or other enhancements that can be chewed off and swallowed. Soft toys that squeak are fun, but a TM puppy can quickly disembowel the toy and remove (and swallow) the squeaker. Toys that rattle or make noise can excite a puppy, but they present the same danger as the squeaky kind and so require supervision. Hard rubber toys that bounce can also entertain a pup, but make sure that the toy is too big for your pup to swallow, like a big log from the woodpile or an old rubber car tire.

puppy crate will be useless. Purchase a crate that will accommodate an adult Tibetan Mastiff; an extra-large crate will be necessary.

BEDDING AND CRATE PADS

Your puppy will enjoy some type of soft bedding in his "room" (the crate), something he can snuggle into to feel cozy and secure. Old towels or blankets are good choices for a young pup, since he may (and probably will) have a toileting accident or two in the crate or decide to chew on the bedding material. Once he is fully trained and out of the early chewing stage, you can replace the puppy bedding with a permanent crate pad if you prefer. Crate pads and other dog beds run the gamut from inexpensive to high-end doggie-designer styles, but don't splurge on the good stuff until you are sure that your puppy is reliable and won't tear it up or make a mess on it.

PUPPY TOYS

Just as infants and older children require objects to stimulate their minds and bodies, puppies need toys to entertain their curious brains, wiggly paws and achy teeth. A fun array of safe doggie toys will help satisfy your puppy's chewing instincts and distract him from gnawing on the leg of your antique chair or your new leather sofa. Most puppy toys are cute and look as if they would

In the swing of things...a litter owned by Richard Eichhorn.

be a lot of fun, but not all are necessarily safe or good for your puppy, so use caution when you go puppy-toy shopping.

Tibetan Mastiff puppies are fairly aggressive chewers and seem to have an affinity for chewing on wood. However, sticks can splinter and break easily and thus are dangerous for them to chew. Only the hardest, strongest toys should be offered to a Tibetan Mastiff. Toys should be large enough so there is no danger of the dog's swallowing them. The best "chewcifiers" are sturdy nylon and hard rubber bones, which are safe to gnaw on

> **THE FAMILY TREE**
> Your puppy's pedigree is his family tree. Just as a child may resemble his parents and grandparents, so too will a puppy reflect the qualities, good and bad, of his ancestors, especially those in the first two generations. Therefore it's important to know as much as possible about a puppy's immediate relatives. Reputable and experienced breeders should be able to explain the pedigree and why they chose to breed from the particular dogs they used.

While a pup enjoys a good toy, he loves little more than his human companions. Here Irene McLuskey cuddles up with puppy Tonka.

and come in sizes appropriate for all age groups and breeds. Be especially careful of natural bones, which can splinter or develop dangerous sharp edges; pups can easily swallow or choke on those bone splinters. Vets often tell of surgical nightmares involving bits of splintered bone, because in addition to the danger of choking, the sharp pieces can damage the intestinal tract.

Similarly, rawhide chews, while a favorite of most dogs and puppies, can be equally dangerous. Pieces of rawhide are easily swallowed after they get soft and gummy from chewing, and dogs have been known to choke on pieces of ingested rawhide. Rawhide chews should be offered only when you can supervise the puppy.

Soft woolly toys, stuffed toys, squeaky toys and toys with small parts (like buttons, eyes, noses) are very easy for a TM pup to destroy and ingest, with the danger of choking or blockages. Braided rope toys are similar in that they are fun to chew and toss around, but they shred easily and the strings are easy to swallow. The strings are not digestible and, if the puppy doesn't pass them in his stool, he could end up at the vet's office. As with rawhides, your puppy should be closely monitored with rope toys.

If you believe that your pup has ingested a piece of one of his toys, check his stools for the next couple of days to see if he passes the item when he defecates. At the same time, also watch for signs of intestinal distress. A call to your veterinarian might be in order to get his advice and be on the safe side.

An all-time favorite toy for puppies (young and old!) is the empty gallon milk jug. Hard plastic juice containers—46 ounces or more—are also excellent. Such containers make lots of noise when they are batted about, and puppies go crazy with delight as they play with them. However, they don't last very long, so be sure to remove and replace them when they get chewed up.

A word of caution about homemade toys: be careful with your choices of non-traditional

Like all TM pups, Basha is cute, curious and resourceful, and needs supervision to stay out of trouble.

play objects. Never use old shoes or socks, since a puppy cannot distinguish between the old ones on which he's allowed to chew and the new ones in your closet that are strictly off limits. That principle applies to anything that resembles something that you don't want your puppy to chew.

COLLARS

A lightweight rolled nylon collar is the best choice for a very young pup. Quick-click collars are easy to put on and remove, and they can be adjusted as the puppy grows. Introduce him to his collar as soon as he comes home to get him accustomed to wearing it. He'll get used to it quickly and won't mind a bit. Make sure that it is snug enough that it won't slip off, yet loose enough to be comfortable for the pup. You should be able to slip two fingers between the collar and his neck. Check the collar often, as puppies grow in spurts, and his collar can become too tight almost overnight. For training, a nylon or metal snake choke collar are recommended for Tibetan Mastiffs.

LEASHES

A 6-foot nylon lead is an excellent choice for a young puppy. It is lightweight and not as tempting to chew as a leather lead. You can switch to a 6-foot leather lead after your pup has grown and is used to walking politely on a lead. For initial puppy walks and house-training purposes, you should invest in a shorter lead so that you have more control over the puppy. At first, you don't want him wandering too far away from you, and when taking him out for toileting you will want to keep him in the specific area chosen for his potty spot.

TOXIC PLANTS

Plants are natural puppy magnets, but many can be harmful, even fatal, if ingested by a puppy or adult dog. Scout your yard and home interior and remove any plants, bushes or flowers that could be even mildly dangerous. It could save your puppy's life. You can obtain a complete list of toxic plants from your veterinarian, at the public library or by looking online.

HOME SAFETY FOR YOUR TIBETAN MASTIFF PUPPY

The importance of puppy-proofing cannot be overstated. In addition to making your house comfortable for your Tibetan Mastiff's arrival, you also must make sure that your house is safe for your puppy before you bring him home. There are countless hazards in the owner's personal living environment that a pup can sniff, chew, swallow or destroy. Many are obvious; others are not. Do a thorough advance house check to remove or rearrange those things that could hurt your puppy, keeping any potentially dangerous items out of areas to which he will have access.

Electrical cords are especially dangerous, since puppies view them as irresistible chew toys. Unplug and remove all exposed cords or fasten them beneath baseboards where the puppy cannot reach them. Veterinarians and firefighters can tell you horror stories about electrical burns and house fires that resulted from puppy-chewed electrical cords. Consider this a most serious precaution for your puppy and the rest of your family.

The Tibetan Mastiff especially likes to chew on anything made of wood—furniture, moldings in the home, trees, boards, etc. Wire can be used around trees to keep the dog away from them, and valuable furniture moved into a room to

A Dog-Safe Home

The dog-safety police are taking you on a house tour. Let's go room by room and see how safe your own home is for your Tibetan Mastiff. The following items are doggy dangers, so either they must be removed or the dog should be monitored or not allowed access to these areas.

LIVING ROOM

- house plants (some varieties are poisonous)
- fireplace or wood-burning stove
- paint on the walls (lead-based paint is toxic)
- lead drapery weights (toxic lead)
- lamps and electrical cords
- carpet cleaners or deodorizers

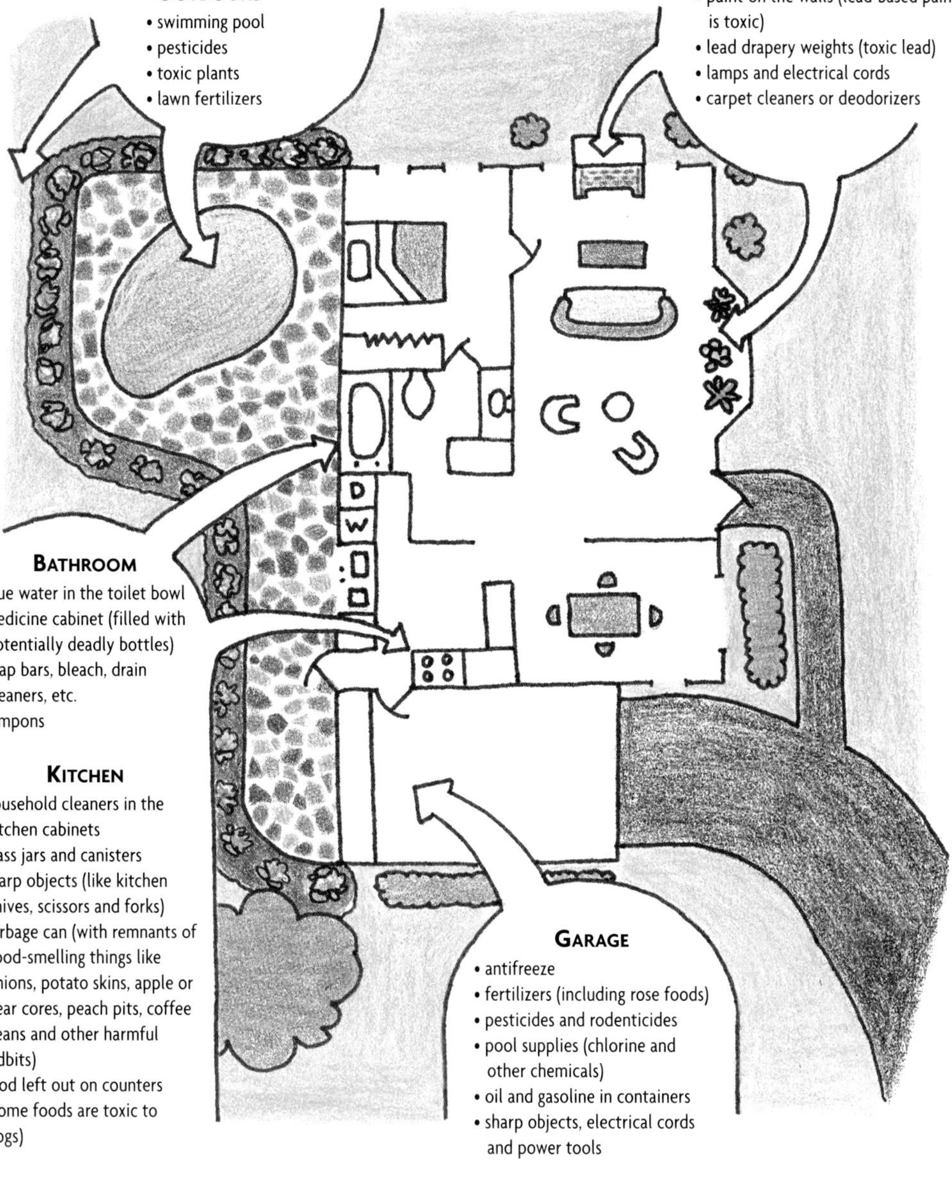

OUTDOORS

- swimming pool
- pesticides
- toxic plants
- lawn fertilizers

BATHROOM

- blue water in the toilet bowl
- medicine cabinet (filled with potentially deadly bottles)
- soap bars, bleach, drain cleaners, etc.
- tampons

KITCHEN

- household cleaners in the kitchen cabinets
- glass jars and canisters
- sharp objects (like kitchen knives, scissors and forks)
- garbage can (with remnants of good-smelling things like onions, potato skins, apple or pear cores, peach pits, coffee beans and other harmful tidbits)
- food left out on counters (some foods are toxic to dogs)

GARAGE

- antifreeze
- fertilizers (including rose foods)
- pesticides and rodenticides
- pool supplies (chlorine and other chemicals)
- oil and gasoline in containers
- sharp objects, electrical cords and power tools

TEETHING TIME

All puppies chew. It's normal canine behavior. Chewing just plain feels good to a puppy, especially during the three- to five-month teething period when the adult teeth are breaking through the gums. Rather than attempting to eliminate such a strong natural chewing instinct, you will be more successful if you redirect it and teach your puppy what he may or may not chew. Correct inappropriate chewing with a sharp "No!" and offer him a chew toy, praising him when he takes it. Don't become discouraged. Chewing usually decreases after the adult teeth have come in.

which the dog does not have access. Also scout your home for tiny objects that might be seen at a pup's eye level. Keep medication bottles and cleaning supplies well out of reach, and do the same with waste baskets and other trash containers. Metal waste baskets and other trash

containers with lids, especially in the kitchen, are recommended. It goes without saying that you should not use rodent poison or other toxic chemicals in any puppy area and that you must keep such containers safely locked up. You will be amazed at how many places a curious puppy can discover!

Once your house has cleared inspection, check your yard. It is recommended that the TM's yard be at least a quarter of an acre, fully fenced. The larger the acreage, the better, always remembering that fencing with this breed is a must. Additional fencing, large rocks, concrete or some other means of preventing digging under the fence is also required. We've mentioned that some TMs are able to jump over high fences; keep this in mind! Asking your breeder about your pup's parents' jumping ability will give you an indication as to how high your pup will be able to jump someday.

Check the fence periodically for necessary repairs. If there is a weak link or space to squeeze through, you can be sure a determined Tibetan Mastiff will discover it. Invisible fencing systems are not recommended for the Tibetan Mastiff. Not only do these systems rarely keep Tibetan Mastiffs in, they do not keep other animals, children or adults from entering the TM's territory.

The garage and shed can be hazardous places for a pup, as things like fertilizers, chemicals and tools are usually kept there. It's best to keep these areas off limits to the pup. Antifreeze is especially dangerous to dogs, as they find the taste appealing and it takes only a few licks from the driveway to kill a dog, puppy or adult, small breed or large.

You may need to use exercise pens or install child gates or another type of barrier to allow your puppy to have his own safe space. The puppy's space should be close to where most of the family action takes place (i.e., the kitchen). As your pup earns more house privileges, his barriers can be moved. A puppy should not have access to stairs until he is several months old.

Many breeders recommend a "double-door" system. Simply stated, this is a system whereby your Tibetan Mastiff would have to get through two barriers (gates, doors, etc.) before escaping from his

safe enclosure. This is especially important for any doorways that lead outside. Many Tibetan Mastiffs are fast and agile, and have been known to bolt through doorways, past their owners and onto roads where they were hit by cars.

VISITING THE VETERINARIAN
A good veterinarian is your Tibetan Mastiff puppy's best health-insurance policy. If you do not already have a vet, ask friends and experienced dog people in your area for recommendations so that you can select a vet, preferably one who knows the breed or at least is experienced with large-breed dogs, before you bring your Tibetan Mastiff puppy home. Also

Alert little guardians Cambu, Tyger and Bangha.

arrange for your puppy's first veterinary examination beforehand, since many vets do not have appointments available immediately and your puppy should visit the vet within a day or so of coming home.

It's important to make sure your puppy's first visit to the vet is a pleasant and positive one. The vet should take great care to befriend the pup and handle him gently to make their first meeting a positive experience. The vet will give the pup a thorough physical examination and set up a schedule for vaccinations and other necessary wellness visits. Be sure to show your vet any health and inoculation records, which you should have received from your breeder. Your vet is a great source of canine health information, so be sure to ask questions and take notes. Creating a health journal for your puppy will make a handy reference for his wellness and any future health problems that may arise.

MEETING THE FAMILY

Your Tibetan Mastiff's homecoming is an exciting time for all members of the family, and it's only natural that everyone will be eager to meet him, pet him and play with him. However, for the puppy's sake, it's best to make these initial family meetings as uneventful as possible so that the pup is not overwhelmed with too much too soon.

> **THE FIRST FAMILY MEETING**
> Your puppy's first week at home should be quiet and uneventful. Despite his wagging tail, he is still wondering where his mom and siblings are! Let him make friends with other members of the family on his own terms; don't overwhelm him. You have a lifetime ahead to get to know each other!

Remember, he has just left his dam and his littermates and is away from the breeder's home for the first time. Despite his fuzzy wagging tail, he is still apprehensive and wondering where he is and who all these strange humans are. It's best to let him explore on his own and meet the family members as he feels comfortable. Let him investigate all the new smells, sights and sounds at his own pace. Children should be especially careful to not get overly excited, use loud voices or hug the pup too tightly. Be calm, gentle and affectionate, and be ready to comfort him if he appears frightened or uneasy.

Be sure to show your puppy his new crate during this first day home. Toss a treat or two inside the crate; if he associates the crate with food, he will associate the crate with good things. If he is comfortable with the crate, you can offer him his first meal inside it. Leave the door ajar so he can wander in and out as he chooses.

FIRST NIGHT IN HIS NEW HOME

So much has happened in your Tibetan Mastiff puppy's first day away from the breeder. He's had his first car ride to his new home. He's met his new human family and perhaps the other family pets. He has explored his new house and yard, at least those places where he is to be allowed during his first weeks at home. He may have visited his new veterinarian. He has eaten his first meal or two away from his dam and littermates. Surely that's enough to tire out an eight-week-old Tibetan Mastiff pup—or so you hope!

It's bedtime. During the day, the pup investigated his crate, which is his new den and sleeping space, so it is not entirely strange to him. Line the crate with a soft towel or blanket that he can snuggle into and gently place him into the crate for the night. Some breeders send home a piece of bedding from where the pup slept with his littermates, and those familiar scents are a great comfort for the puppy on his first night without his siblings.

He will probably whine or cry. The puppy is objecting to the confinement and the fact that he is alone for the first time. This can be a stressful time for you as well as for the pup. It's important that you remain strong and don't let the puppy out of his crate to comfort him. He will fall asleep eventually. If you release him, the puppy will learn that crying means "out" and will continue that habit. You are laying the groundwork for future habits. Some breeders find that soft music can soothe a crying pup and help him get to sleep.

TM puppies grow quickly. Four-month-old Pretty is catching up in size to ten-year-old Ernie!

Two things that Tibetan Mastiffs love: cold weather and the company of other TMs. Here are Cakra, Senge and Rewa in the Czech Republic.

DIGGING OUT

Tibetan Mastiffs love to dig! Digging is considered "self-rewarding behavior" because it's fun! Of all the digging solutions offered by the experts, most are only marginally successful and none is guaranteed to work. The best cure is prevention, which means removing the dog from the offending site when he digs as well as distracting him when you catch him digging so that he turns his attentions elsewhere. That means that you have to supervise your dog's yard time. An unsupervised digger can create havoc with your landscaping or, worse, run away! The best deterrent for the TM is an electric hotwire along the base of the fenceline.

SOCIALIZING YOUR PUPPY

Because the Tibetan Mastiff is a guarding breed, instinct can make them aggressive with other dogs that they consider a threat. Socialization will help him become well adjusted as he grows up and less prone to being aggressive toward, timid about or fearful of the new things he will encounter. The first 20 weeks of your Tibetan Mastiff puppy's life are the most important of his entire lifetime. A properly socialized puppy will grow up to be a confident and stable adult who will be a pleasure to live with and a welcome addition to the neighborhood.

The importance of socialization cannot be overemphasized. Research on canine behavior has proven that puppies of any breed who are not exposed to new sights, sounds, people and animals during their first 20 weeks of life will grow up to be timid and fearful, even aggressive, and unable to flourish outside of their home environment.

Socializing your puppy is not difficult and, in fact, will be a fun time for you both. Lead training goes hand in hand with socialization, so your puppy will be learning how to walk on a lead at the same time that he's meeting the neighborhood. Because the Tibetan Mastiff is such a terrific breed, everyone will enjoy meeting "the new kid on the block." Take him for short walks, to the park and to other dog-friendly places where he will encounter new people, especially children. Puppies automatically recognize children as "little people" and are drawn to play

Sharing a homeland—and a stick—are Tibetan Terrier Kasar and Tibetan Mastiff Burma.

with them. Just make sure that you supervise these meetings and that the children do not get too rough or encourage him to play too hard. An overzealous pup can often nip too hard, frightening the child and in turn making the puppy overly excited. A bad experience in puppyhood can impact a dog for life, so a pup that has a negative experience with a child may grow up to be shy or even aggressive around children.

Take your puppy along on your daily errands. Puppies are natural "people magnets," and most people who see your pup will want to pet him. All of these encounters will help to mold him into a confident adult dog. Likewise, you will soon feel like a confident, responsible dog owner, rightly proud of your handsome Tibetan Mastiff.

Be especially careful of your puppy's encounters and experiences during the eight-to-ten-week-old period, which is also called the "fear period." This is a serious imprinting period, and all contact during this time should be gentle and positive. A frightening or negative event could leave a permanent impression that could affect his future behavior if a similar situation arises.

Also make sure that your puppy has received his first and second rounds of vaccinations before you expose him to other dogs or bring him to places that other dogs may frequent. Avoid dog parks and other strange-dog areas until your vet assures you that your puppy is fully immunized and resistant to the diseases that can be passed between canines. Discuss safe early socialization with your breeder and vet, as some recommend socializing the puppy even before he has received all of his inoculations.

LEADER OF THE PUPPY'S PACK
Like other canines, your puppy needs an authority figure, someone he can look up to and regard as the leader of his "pack." His first pack leader was his dam, who taught him to be polite and not to chew too hard on her ears or nip

Socialization is a family affair in this pack: Wayne Scot Lukas with adult TM Titus and puppy Elsa.

Roughhousing with siblings is a favorite puppy pastime and also very educational in teaching pups how to interact with other canines.

at her muzzle. He learned those same lessons from his littermates. If he played too rough, they cried in pain and stopped the game, which sent an important message to the rowdy puppy.

As puppies play together, they are also struggling to determine who will be the boss. Being pack animals, dogs need someone to be in charge. If a litter of puppies remained together beyond puppyhood, one of the pups would emerge as the strongest one, the one who calls the shots.

Once your puppy leaves the pack, he will look intuitively for a new leader. If he does not recognize you as that leader, he will try to assume that position for himself. Of course, it is hard to imagine your adorable Tibetan Mastiff puppy trying to be in charge when he is so small and seemingly helpless. You must remember that these are natural canine instincts. Do not cave in and allow your pup to get the upper "paw"!

Just as socialization is so important during these first 20 weeks, so too is your puppy's early education. He was born without any bad habits. He does not know what is good or bad behavior. If he does things like nipping and digging, it's because he is having fun and doesn't know that humans consider these things as "bad." It's your job to teach him proper puppy manners, and this is the best time to accomplish that—before he has developed bad habits, since it is much more difficult to "unlearn" or correct unacceptable learned behavior than to teach good behavior from the start.

Make sure that all members of the family understand the importance of being consistent when training their new puppy. If you tell the puppy to stay off the sofa and your daughter allows him to cuddle on the couch to watch her favorite television show, your pup will be confused about what he is and is not allowed to do. Have a family conference before

> **REPEAT YOURSELF**
> Puppies learn best through repetition. Use the same verbal cues and commands when teaching your puppy new behaviors or correcting for misbehaviors. Be consistent, but not monotonous. Puppies get bored just like puppy owners, and TMs are among the smartest and most stubborn of breeds.

your pup comes home so that everyone understands the basic principles of puppy training and the rules you have set forth for the pup, and agrees to follow them.

The old saying that "an ounce of prevention is worth a pound of cure" is especially true when it comes to puppies. It is much easier to prevent inappropriate behavior than it is to change it. It's also easier and less stressful for the pup, since it will keep discipline to a minimum and create a more positive learning environment for him. That, in turn, will also be easier on you!

Here are a few commonsense tips to keep your belongings safe and your puppy out of trouble:

- Keep your closet doors closed and your shoes, socks and other apparel off the floor so your puppy can't get at them.
- Keep a secure lid on the trash container or put the trash where your puppy can't dig into it. He can't damage what he can't reach!
- Supervise your puppy at all times to make sure he is not getting into mischief. If he starts to chew the corner of the rug, you can distract him instantly by tossing a toy for him to fetch. You also will be able to whisk him outside when you notice that he is about to piddle on the carpet. If you can't see your puppy, you can't teach him or correct his behavior.

WATCH THE WATER
To help your puppy sleep through the night without having to relieve himself, remove his water bowl after 7 p.m. Offer him a couple of ice cubes during the evening to quench his thirst. Never leave water in a puppy's crate, as this is inviting puddles of mishaps.

SOLVING PUPPY PROBLEMS

CHEWING AND NIPPING
Nipping at fingers and toes is normal puppy behavior. Chewing is also the way that puppies investigate their surroundings. However, you will have to teach your puppy that chewing anything other than his toys is not acceptable. That won't happen overnight and at times puppy teeth will test your patience. However, if you allow nipping and chewing to continue, just think about the damage that a Tibetan Mastiff puppy or adult can do.

Whenever your puppy nips your hand or fingers, cry out

Pabu keeps a watchful eye on eight-week-old Basha as she explores her new world.

to handle it themselves, you may have to intervene. Puppy nips can be quite painful and a child's frightened reaction will only encourage a puppy to nip harder, which is a natural canine response. As with all other puppy situations, interaction between your TM puppy and children should be supervised.

Chewing on objects, not just family members' fingers and ankles, is also normal canine behavior that can be especially tedious (for the owner, not the pup) during the teething period when the puppy's adult teeth are coming in. At this stage, chewing just plain feels good. Furniture legs and cabinet corners are common puppy favorites. Shoes and other personal items also taste pretty good to a pup.

The best solution is, once again, prevention. If you value something, keep it tucked away and out of reach. You can't hide your dining-room table in a closet, but you can try to deflect the chewing by applying a bitter product made just to deter dogs from chewing. This spray-on substance is vile-tasting, although safe for dogs, and most puppies will avoid the forbidden object after one tiny taste. You also can apply the product to your leather leash if the puppy tries to chew on his lead during leash-training sessions.

Keep a ready supply of safe chews handy to offer your Tibetan Mastiff as a distraction when he starts to chew on something that's a

"Ouch!" in a loud voice, which should startle your puppy and stop him from nipping, even if only for a moment. Immediately distract him by offering a small treat or an appropriate toy for him to chew instead (which means having chew toys and puppy treats handy or in your pockets at all times). Praise him when he takes the toy and tell him what a good fellow he is. Praise is just as or even more important in puppy training as discipline and correction.

Puppies also tend to nip at children more often than adults, since they perceive little ones to be more vulnerable and more similar to their littermates. Teach your children appropriate responses to nipping behavior. If they are unable "no-no." Remember, at this tender age he does not yet know what is permitted or forbidden, so you have to be "on call" every minute he's awake and on the prowl.

You may lose a treasure or two during puppy's growing-up period, and the furniture could sustain a nasty nick or two. These can be trying times, so be prepared for those inevitable accidents and comfort yourself in knowing that this too shall pass.

JUMPING UP

Puppies will be puppies, and puppies jump up—on you, your guests, your counters and your furniture. Just another normal part of growing up, and one you need to meet head-on before it becomes an ingrained habit and you have over 100 pounds of Tibetan Mastiff jumping up to say hello.

BE CONSISTENT

Consistency is a key element, in fact is absolutely necessary, to a puppy's learning environment. A behavior (such as chewing, jumping up or climbing onto the furniture) cannot be forbidden one day and then allowed the next. That will only confuse the pup, and he will not understand what he is supposed to do. Just one or two episodes of allowing an undesirable behavior to "slide" will imprint that behavior on a puppy's brain and make that behavior more difficult to erase or change.

The key to jump correction is consistency. You cannot correct your Tibetan Mastiff for jumping up on you today, then allow it to happen tomorrow by greeting him with hugs and kisses. As you have learned by now, consistency is critical to all puppy lessons.

For starters, try turning your back as soon as the puppy jumps. Jumping up is a means of gaining your attention and, if the pup can't see your face, he may get discouraged and learn that he loses eye contact with his beloved master when he jumps up.

Leash corrections also work, and most puppies respond well to a leash tug if they jump. Grasp the leash close to the puppy's collar and give a quick tug downward, using the command "Off." Do not use the word "Down," since "Down" is used to teach the puppy to lie down, which is a separate action that he will learn during his education in the basic commands. As soon as the puppy has backed off, tell him to sit and immediately praise him for doing so. This will take many repetitions and won't be accomplished quickly, so don't get discouraged or give up; you must be even more persistent than your puppy.

Another method used for jump correction is the spritzer bottle. Fill a spray bottle with water mixed with a bit of lemon juice or vinegar. As soon as puppy jumps, command him "Off" and spritz him with the water mixture. Of course, that means having the spray bottle handy whenever or wherever jumping usually happens.

Yet another method to discourage jumping is grasping the puppy's paws and holding them gently but firmly until he struggles to get away. Wait a brief moment or two, then release his paws and give him a command to sit. He should eventually learn that jumping gets him into an uncomfortable predicament.

Children are major victims of puppy jumping, since puppies view little people as ready targets for jumping up as well as nipping. If your children (or their friends) are unable to dispense jump corrections, you will have to intervene and handle it for them.

Important to prevention is also knowing what you should not do. Never kick your Tibetan Mastiff (for any reason, not just for jumping) or knock him in the chest with your knee. That maneuver could actually harm your puppy. Vets can tell you stories about puppies who suffered broken bones after being banged about when they jumped up.

PUPPY WHINING
Puppies often cry and whine, just as infants and little children do. It's their way of telling us that they are lonely or in need of attention. Your puppy will miss his littermates and will feel insecure when he is left alone. You may be out of the house

or just in another room, but he will still feel alone. During these times, the puppy's crate should be his personal comfort station, a place all his own where he can feel safe and secure. Once he learns that being alone is okay and not something to be feared, he will settle down without crying or objecting. You might want to leave a radio on while he is crated, as the sound of human voices can be soothing and will give the impression that people are around.

Give your puppy a favorite sturdy chew toy to entertain him whenever he is crated. You will both be happier: the puppy because he is safe in his den and you because he is quiet, safe and not getting into puppy escapades that can wreak havoc in your house or cause him danger.

To make sure that your puppy will always view his crate as a safe and cozy place, never, ever use the crate as punishment. That's the best way to turn the crate into a negative place that the pup will want to avoid. Sure, you can use the crate for your own peace of mind if your puppy is getting into trouble and needs some "time out." Just don't let him know that! Never scold the pup and immediately place him into the crate. Count to ten, give him a couple of hugs and maybe a treat, then scoot him into his crate.

It's also important not to make a big fuss when he is released from the crate. That will make getting out of the crate more appealing than being in the crate, which is just the opposite of what you are trying to achieve.

"COUNTER SURFING"

What we like to call "counter surfing" is a normal extension of jumping and usually starts to happen as soon as a puppy realizes that he is big enough to stand on his hind legs and investigate the good stuff on the kitchen counter or the coffee table. Once again, you have to be there to prevent it! As soon as you see your Tibetan Mastiff even start to raise himself up, startle him with a sharp "No!" or "Aaahh, aaahh!" If he succeeds and manages to get one or both paws on the forbidden surface, lower him gently to the ground while telling him "Off!" As soon as he's back on all four paws, command him to sit and praise at once.

For surf prevention, make sure to keep any tempting treats or edibles out of reach, where your Tibetan Mastiff can't see or smell them. It's the old rule of prevention yet again.

FOOD AND TOY GUARDING

Some dogs are picky eaters; others seem to inhale their food without chewing it. Occasionally, the true "chow hound" will become protective of his food, which is one dangerous step toward other aggressive behavior. Food guarding is obvious: your puppy will growl, snarl or even attempt to bite you if you approach his food bowl or put your hand into his pan while he's eating.

This behavior is not acceptable, and very preventable! If your puppy is an especially voracious eater, sit next to him occasionally while he eats and dangle your fingers in his food bowl or hand feed him. Don't feed him in a corner, where he could feel possessive of his eating space. Rather, place his food bowl in an open area of your kitchen where you are in close proximity. Occasionally remove his food in mid-meal, tell him he's a good boy and return his bowl.

If your pup becomes possessive of his food, look for other signs of future aggression, like guarding his favorite toys or refusing to obey obedience commands that he knows. Consult an obedience trainer for help in reinforcing obedience so your TM will fully understand that *you* are the boss. Your Tibetan Mastiff must learn that all good things come from his owners.

HAPPY PUPPIES COME RUNNING
Never call your puppy (or adult dog) to come to you and then scold him or discipline him when he gets there. He will make a natural association between coming to you and being scolded, and he will think he was a bad dog for coming to you. He will then be reluctant to come whenever he is called. Always praise your puppy every time he comes to you.

PROPER CARE OF YOUR

TIBETAN MASTIFF

FEEDING

SPECIAL FEEDING CONSIDERATIONS

A Tibetan Mastiff puppy will grow rapidly and should therefore be fed sensibly on a high-quality diet. However, an owner should never be tempted to allow the puppy to put on too much weight, as this will play havoc with his construction during the period of bone growth. Indeed, even in adulthood, a Tibetan Mastiff should not be allowed to carry too much weight, for a dog that is overweight is much more likely to suffer health problems.

That being said, something inside the make-up of the Tibetan Mastiff seems to tell him how much food is required, so that overfeeding is not usually a problem. This may well be something passed down from their ancestors; indeed, even today, in the breed's natural habitat, food is rarely in plentiful supply.

Adults of both sexes will also think nothing of regurgitating food for puppies. This is never a pleasant sight for the human onlooker, but food that has been regurgitated has not been fully

digested so is still full of nutrients and can do no harm. It is instinctive in bitches of many breeds, but for males to do this is quite unusual. Again the survival instinct seems to come to the fore.

In its natural habitat, the Tibetan Mastiff eats very little protein, so selection of a diet that is low in protein is generally most suitable for this breed. The Tibetan

---

NOT HUNGRY?
While TM puppies will eat you out of house and home, adult TMs are usually rather light eaters. However, if you notice that your dog has lost interest in his food, there could be any number of causes. Dental problems are a common cause of appetite loss, one that is often overlooked. If your dog has a toothache, a loose tooth or sore gums from infection, chances are it doesn't feel so good to chew. Think about when you've had a toothache! If your dog does not approach the food bowl with his usual enthusiasm, look inside his mouth for signs of a problem. Whatever the cause, you'll want to consult your vet so that your TM can get back to his happy, healthy self as soon as possible.

SWITCHING FOODS

There are certain times in a dog's life when it becomes necessary to switch his food; for example, from puppy to adult food and then from adult to senior-dog food. Additionally, you may decide to feed your pup a different type of food from what he received from the breeder, and there may be "emergency" situations in which you can't find your dog's normal brand and have to offer something else temporarily. Anytime a change is made, for whatever reason, the switch must be done gradually. You don't want to upset the dog's stomach or end up with a picky eater who refuses to eat something new. A tried-and-true approach is, over the course of about a week, to mix a little of the new food in with the old, increasing the proportion of new to old as the days progress. At the end of the week, you'll be feeding his regular portions of the new food, and he will barely notice the change.

may be special situations in which pups fail to nurse, necessitating that the breeder hand-feed them with a formula, but for the most part pups spend the first weeks of life nursing from their dam. The breeder weans the pups by gradually introducing solid foods and decreasing the milk meals. Pups may even start themselves off on the weaning process, albeit inadvertently, if they snatch bites from their mom's food bowl.

By the time the pups are ready for new homes, they are fully weaned and eating a good puppy food. As a new owner, you may be thinking, "Great! The breeder has taken care of the hard part." Not so fast.

A puppy's first year of life is the time when all or most of his growth and development takes place. This is a delicate time, and diet plays a huge role in proper skeletal and muscular formation.

Nursing her hungry litter is a labor of love for this devoted mom.

Mastiff has an ability to absorb thoroughly all the nutrients in its diet, the result being that fecal material is small in quantity in comparison with dogs of similar size. The breed also enjoys fruit, though one should be sure to remove any pits so that these are not swallowed inadvertently.

FEEDING THE PUPPY

Of course, your pup's very first food will be his dam's milk. There

DIET DON'TS

- Got milk? Don't give it to your dog unless it's goat's milk! Dogs cannot tolerate large quantities of cows' milk, as they do not have the enzymes to digest lactose.
- You may have heard of dog owners who add raw eggs to their dogs' food for a shiny coat or to make the food more palatable, but consumption of raw eggs too often can cause a deficiency of the vitamin biotin. Stick with hard-boiled eggs.
- Avoid feeding table scraps, as they will upset the balance of the dog's complete food. Additionally, fatty or highly seasoned foods can cause upset canine stomachs.
- If you offer raw meat to your dog, make sure it is fresh and combine it with a balanced diet.
- Vitamin A toxicity in dogs can be caused by too much raw liver, especially if the dog already gets enough vitamin A in his balanced diet, which should be the case.
- Bones like chicken, pork chop and other soft bones are not suitable, as they easily splinter, but a big raw beef knuckle or leg bone is recommended.

Improper diet and exercise habits can lead to damaging problems that will compromise the dog's health and movement for his entire life. That being said, new owners should not worry needlessly. With the myriad types of food formulated specifically for growing pups of different-sized breeds, dog-food manufacturers have taken much of the guesswork out of feeding your puppy well. Feed a high-quality large-breed puppy food with less than 12% calcium content. Since puppy-food formulas are designed to provide the nutrition that a growing puppy needs, it is unnecessary and, in fact, can prove harmful to add supplements to the diet. Research has shown that too much of certain vitamin supplements and minerals, especially calcium, predispose a dog to skeletal problems. It's by no means a case of "if a little is good, a lot is better." At every stage of your dog's life, too much or too little in the way of nutrients can be harmful, which is why a manufactured complete food is the easiest way to know that your dog is getting what he needs.

Because of a young pup's small body and accordingly small digestive system, his daily portion will be divided up into small meals throughout the day. This can mean starting off with three or even more meals a day. Feeding the pup at the same times and in the same place each day is important for both housebreaking purposes and establishing the dog's everyday routine. Even as an adult, a Tibetan Mastiff should stay on a three-meal-per-day feeding schedule as a preventive measure to guard against bloat, with no exercise within the hour before and after meals.

Free-choice feeding is not recommended as, in addition to increasing the risk of bloat, it may lead to excess calories, resulting in rapid growth and excess weight gain.

The adult size of your Tibetan Mastiff is determined primarily by the size of his parents. Increasing

THE DARK SIDE OF CHOCOLATE

From a tiny chip to a giant rabbit, chocolate—in any form—is not your dog's friend. Whether it's an Oreo® cookie, a Snickers® bar or even a couple of M&M's®, you should avoid these items with your dog. You are also well advised to avoid any bone toy that is made out of fake chocolate or any treat made of carob—anything that encourages your dog to become a "chocoholic" can't be helpful. Before you toss your pooch half of your candy bar, consider that as little as a single ounce of chocolate can poison a 30-pound dog. Theobromine, like caffeine, is a methylxanthine and occurs naturally in cocoa beans. Dogs metabolize theobromine very slowly, and its effect on the dog can be serious, harming the heart, kidneys and central nervous system. Dark or semi-sweet chocolate is even worse than milk chocolate, and baking chocolate and cocoa mix are by far the worst.

the calorie intake of a puppy will only increase the rate at which the puppy gains weight. The slower-growing puppy will eventually weigh the same as an adult and is less likely to develop joint and bone problems.

Watch your pup's weight as he grows and, if the recommended amounts seem to be too much or too little for your pup, consult the vet about appropriate dietary changes. Keep in mind that treats, although small, can quickly add up throughout the day, contributing unnecessary calories. Treats are fine when used prudently; opt for dog treats

The breeder will slowly wean the litter off mom's milk and onto a suitable solid food.

BLOAT AND THE TIBETAN MASTIFF

Bloat (gastric torsion/dilatation), although uncommon in this breed, can prove fatal in the Tibetan Mastiff and is an emergency that requires immediate attention. This is a condition to which large, deep-chested dogs are most prone, although no dog is immune. It has many and varied causes; some common ones include swallowing air during exercise, gulping food and/or water, exercising too close to mealtimes and stress, especially stress or over-excitement at mealtimes.

The stomach of an affected dog twists, restricting the flow of food and blood. This causes gas to build up in the stomach and toxins to build up in the bloodstream. Shock quickly follows and death soon after if left untreated. The dog may cry, dry-heave, strain in an attempt to defecate, refuse to walk or lie down and/or exhibit other symptoms. The dog's abdomen will become hardened and will be sensitive to touch; the dog may even growl or snap at someone who touches his abdomen.

The best preventive measures seem to be not allowing moderate to heavy exercise after eating, feeding three small meals a day (food moistened with water) instead of one large meal (to prevent gulping air) and not allowing the dog to get stressed or excited at and after mealtimes. Discuss further preventive measures with your breeder and veterinarian.

specially formulated to be healthy or for nutritious snacks like small pieces of dried liver or cooked chicken.

When you buy your puppy, the breeder should have provided you with a diet sheet giving details of exactly how your puppy has been fed. If you have chosen your breeder well, you should be able to obtain sound advice from that breeder as to which food is considered most suitable. Some breeders feel their dogs thrive best on a wheat-based diet. You will also get advice on amounts to feed, and how and when to switch to an adult-maintenance diet.

FEEDING THE ADULT DOG

For the adult (meaning physically mature) dog, feeding properly is about maintenance, not growth. A Tibetan Mastiff will reach its full height during puppyhood, but continues to develop physically for much longer—bitches until between two and three years of age, and dogs up to at least four years old. Depending on the brand of food used, generally you can switch your Tibetan Mastiff to an adult diet by about 10 or 11 months of age.

Again, correct weight is a concern. Your dog should appear fit and should have an evident "waist." His ribs should not be protruding (a sign of being underweight), but they should be covered by only a slight layer of fat. Under normal circumstances, an adult dog can be maintained fairly easily with a high-quality nutritionally complete adult-formula food.

Factor treats into your dog's overall daily caloric intake, and avoid offering table scraps. Certain "people foods," such as chocolate, grapes, raisins, nuts, onions and quantities of garlic, are toxic to dogs; feeding table scraps also encourages begging and overeating. Overweight dogs are more prone to health problems. Research has even shown that obesity takes years off a dog's life. With that in mind, resist the urge to overfeed and over-treat. Don't make unnecessary additions to your dog's diet, whether with tidbits or with extra vitamins and minerals.

The amount of food needed for proper maintenance will vary depending on the individual dog's activity level, but you will be able to tell whether the daily portions are keeping him in good shape. With the wide variety of good complete foods available, choosing what to feed is largely a matter of personal preference. Just as with the puppy, the adult dog should have consistency in his mealtimes and feeding place. In addition to a consistent routine, regular mealtimes also allow the owner to see how much his dog is eating. If the dog seems never to be satisfied or, likewise, becomes uninterested in his food, the

EASY, COWBOY!

Who's going to convince your dog that his rawhide toy isn't food? Dogs love rawhide and usually masticate the hide until it's soft enough to swallow, which can lead to choking or intestinal blockage. Another possible danger of rawhide results from the hides used in certain countries. Foreign hides can contain arsenic, lead, antibiotics or *Salmonella* bacilli. Even though imported chews are usually cheaper than American-made chews, this is one example in which buying American really counts. Owners must carefully observe their dogs when they are chewing rawhide and remove any soft pieces that the dog pulls from the hide. Despite these drawbacks, rawhide chews do offer some benefits. Chewing rawhide can help keep the dog's teeth clean and distract your dog from chewing on your favorite leather loafers or sofa. You can also use chew hooves or large beef bones instead.

owner will know right away that something is wrong and can consult the vet. Set feeding times also allow you to practice important bloat preventives, such as giving your Tibetan Mastiff adequate resting time before and after meals and making sure he does not eat too quickly.

DIETS FOR THE AGING DOG

Your Tibetan Mastiff will be considered a senior at about 7 years of age; he has a projected lifespan of between 8 to 14 years, and some live even longer. Senior status varies from breed to breed, with larger breeds being considered seniors at an earlier age than smaller breeds.

What does aging have to do with your dog's diet? No, he won't get a discount at the local diner's early-bird special. Yes, he will require some dietary changes to accommodate the changes that

There's no mistaking that Charlie is ready for dinner!

come along with increased age. One change is that the older dog's dietary needs become more similar to that of a puppy. Specifically, dogs can metabolize more protein as seniors than in the adult-maintenance stage. Discuss with your vet whether you need to switch to a higher-protein or senior-formulated food or whether your current adult-dog food contains sufficient nutrition for the senior. Although some Tibetan Mastiff owners do not find it necessary to switch to a senior diet, age-related factors can often be handled with a change in diet and a change in feeding schedule to give smaller portions that are more easily digested.

Watching the dog's weight remains essential, even more so in the senior stage. Older dogs are already more vulnerable to illness, and obesity only contributes to their susceptibility to problems. As the older dog becomes less active and, thus, exercises less, his regular portions may cause him to gain weight. At this point, you may consider decreasing his daily food intake or switching to a reduced-calorie food. As with other changes, you should consult your vet for advice.

TYPES OF FOOD AND READING THE LABEL

When selecting the type of food to feed your dog, it is important to check out the label for ingredients. Many dry-food products have soybean, corn or rice as the main ingredient. The main ingredient will be listed first on the label, with the rest of the ingredients following in descending order according to their proportion in the food. While these types of dry food are fine, you should also look into dry foods based on meat or fish. These are better-quality foods and thus higher priced. However, they may be just as economical in the long run, because studies have shown that it takes less of the higher-quality foods to maintain a dog.

Comparing the various types of dog food, dry, canned and semi-moist, dry foods contain the least amount of water and canned foods the most. Proportionately, dry foods are the most calorie- and nutrient-dense, which means that you need more of a canned food product to supply the same amount of nutrition. In households with breeds of different sizes, the canned/dry/semi-moist question can be of special importance. Larger breeds obviously eat more than smaller ones and thus in general do better on dry foods, but smaller breeds do fine on canned foods and require "small bite" formulations to protect their small mouths and teeth if fed dry foods. So if you have breeds of different sizes consider both your own prefer-ences and what your dogs like to

There's nothing like a big bowl of cool fresh water for a big puppy.

eat, but mainly think canned for the little guys and dry or semi-moist for everyone else. You may find success mixing the food types as well. Water is important for all dogs, but even more so for those fed dry foods, as there is no high water content in their food.

There are strict controls that regulate the nutritional content of dog food, and a food has to meet the minimum requirements in order to be considered "complete and balanced." It is important that you choose such a food for your dog, so check the label to be sure that your chosen food meets the requirements. If not, look for a food that clearly states on the label that it is formulated to be complete and balanced for your dog's particular stage of life.

Recommendations for amounts to feed will also be indicated on the label. You should also ask your vet about proper food portions, and you will keep an eye on your dog's condition to see whether the recommended amounts are adequate. If he becomes over- or underweight, you will need to make adjustments; this also would be a good time to consult your vet.

The food label may also make feeding suggestions, such as whether moistening a dry-food product is recommended. For the TM, adding water to the dog's food is especially important when it is hot, dry or very cold in the dog's environment, but also is recommended as a daily bloat preventive. Further, sometimes a splash of water will make the food more palatable for the dog or slow down a quick eater. Don't be overwhelmed by the many factors that go into feeding your dog. Manufacturers of complete and balanced foods make it easy, and once you find the right food and amounts for your Tibetan Mastiff, his daily feeding will be a matter of routine.

DON'T FORGET THE WATER!
For a dog, it's always time for a drink! Regardless of what type of food he eats, there's no doubt that he needs plenty of water. Fresh cold water, in a clean bowl, should be freely available to your dog at all times. Due to the chemicals in treated water, spring water is preferred. There are

special circumstances, such as during puppy housebreaking, when you will want to monitor your pup's water intake so that you will be able to predict when he will need to relieve himself, but water must be available to him nonetheless. Water is essential for hydration and proper body function just as it is in humans.

You will get to know how much your dog typically drinks in a day. Of course, in the heat or if exercising vigorously, he will be more thirsty and will drink more. However, if he begins to drink noticeably more water for no apparent reason, this could signal any of various problems, and you are advised to consult your vet.

Water is the best drink for dogs. Some owners are tempted to give milk from time to time or to moisten dry food with milk, but dogs do not have the enzymes necessary to digest the lactose in milk, which is much different from the milk that nursing puppies receive. Therefore, stick with clean fresh water to quench your dog's thirst, and always have it readily available to him.

A word of caution concerning your deep-chested dog's water intake: he should never be allowed to gulp water, especially at mealtimes. In fact, his water intake should be limited at mealtimes as a rule. This simple daily precaution can go a long way in protecting your dog from the dangerous and potentially fatal gastric torsion (bloat).

EXERCISE

Fully adult Tibetan Mastiffs are very capable of walking for miles each day if their owners have the time and stamina. However, until the age of one year, exercise should be restricted, as this is the period of fastest bone growth in this large breed. Puppies should never be taken on long walks, and they should be given plenty of time to rest between short periods of play. However, as they reach adulthood, exercise can gradually be increased, and an adult Tibetan Mastiff in fit condition will accept as much exercise as you wish to give.

Looking back over the years, a Tibetan Mastiff that always stands out in my mind as having had extremely strong hindquarters is one from an early litter born in the UK. His owner was a great hill walker who took his dog with him everywhere. This clearly paid dividends, and the dog lived to a ripe old age.

The TM's muscles need to be kept in good, firm condition and exercise, even walking on lead, stimulates not only the muscles but also the mind. Always remember that your Tibetan Mastiff is a member of a large breed with guarding instincts, and so should only be let off lead in

These TM friends enjoy a good romp in invigorating weather.

securely enclosed areas where you are entirely certain that he can come to no harm and can do no harm to others.

Although Tibetan Mastiffs enjoy living indoors, your dog should have a fenced yard to exercise in or a designated fenced area of the yard. This area should be secure and regularly checked, always keeping in mind that this breed loves to chew at wood. Owners should also keep in mind that if a Tibetan Mastiff is given his own personal "space," he will usually display a strong instinct to guard it. After all, it is his territory!

GROOMING

BASIC COAT MAINTENANCE

The best time to start a grooming routine is as soon as you acquire your pup. If grooming time is made a routine from puppyhood, you and your TM will find that this is a wonderfully relaxing time that is equally enjoyable for both of you. Grooming should be done in a non-stressful environment, without time constraints if possible. Basic grooming tools for your TM are large nail clippers, a large pin brush, a medium to fine metal comb, a dematting rake and possibly a slicker brush for the finishing touches.

Grooming also is an excellent step in preventive medicine. It is during this hands-on grooming time that you can detect small problems and have them assessed before they become big (and often expensive) problems. Checking for hot spots, tooth decay, eye infections, parasites, lumps, cuts, embedded thorns, debris in the coat, etc., as well as assessing the overall condition of the ears, skin, coat, eyes, footpads and rest of

Despite the abundance of coat, Tibetan Mastiffs only require weekly brushing to keep their coats mat- and tangle-free. Quality brushes can be purchased from your pet-supply shop.

your TM's body are all essential for keeping your dog comfortable, happy and in good health. If you and your TM are city dwellers, you will want to check for things like asphalt, tar, gum, glass and the like stuck in his pads. If you are in the country, you will want to check for burs, sticks, seeds, molds, thorns or anything else in the environ-ment that may endanger the comfort or health of your TM. Further, with a male dog, you will want to check his penis and sheath for signs of inflammation or infection. With a female, you will want to check the vaginal opening for signs of infection (especially if your female is in heat), especially foul-smelling discharge.

The TM is a double-coated breed. The breed's outer coat consists of longer, straight, coarse hairs (especially along the spine, hackles and "mane"), and the thick undercoat may range from a cottony to a woolly consistency. Some TMs carry a much denser coat than others and are more prone than other TMs to matting. Once per year (usually in the spring), the Tibetan Mastiff will "blow coat." This means that the undercoat will come out profusely in large clumps. Daily brushing/ combing during this time is recommended.

For the rest of the year, weekly brushing should maintain the TM's coat in good condition. When brushing or combing, start

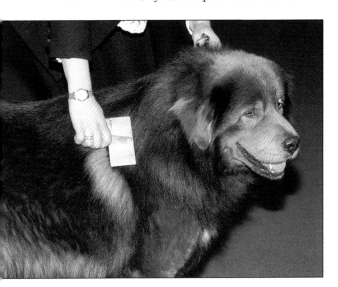

On either side of the lens, Black Princess, Senge and Rewa are picture-perfect.

at the bottom of the legs and work upwards. Brush out the body from back to front, ensuring that you are getting down to the skin and moving outwards. When finished, your TM will shake and his fur will naturally fall into place beautifully.

If mats occur, small mats may be taken out with a dematting comb. Using baby powder on medium-sized mats, rubbing it through and then using a slicker brush to demat, is also a good technique to remove mats. Larger mats will need a dematting rake. Common areas for matting are behind the ears, the feathering of the front and rear legs, the tail plume and under the arms. Clipping or shearing the TM's coat to keep the dog cool in the summer is not recommended, as the breed's

coat acts as an insulator in both the summer and the winter months. A show dog's coat should never be trimmed except to neaten up the feet.

BATHING

In general, dogs need to be bathed only a few times a year, possibly more often if your dog gets into something messy or if he starts to smell like a dog. Show dogs are usually bathed before every show, which could be as frequent as weekly, although this depends on the owner. Bathing too frequently can have negative effects on the skin and coat, removing natural oils and causing dryness.

If you give your dog his first bath when he is young, he will become accustomed to the process. Wrestling a dog into the tub or chasing a freshly shampooed dog who has escaped from the bath will be no fun! Most dogs don't naturally enjoy their baths, but you at least want yours to cooperate with you.

Before bathing the dog, have the items you'll need close at hand. First, decide where you will bathe the dog. You should have a tub or basin with a non-slip surface. Young puppies can even be bathed in a sink. In warm weather, some like to use a portable pool in the yard, although you'll want to make sure your dog doesn't head for the nearest dirt pile following his

bath! You will also need a hose or shower spray to wet the coat thoroughly, a shampoo formulated for dogs, absorbent towels and perhaps a blow dryer. Human shampoos are too harsh for dogs' coats and will dry them out.

Before wetting the dog, give him a comb-through to remove any dead hair, dirt and mats. Any mats left in the coat will "felt" when wet and become much more difficult to remove. Make sure he is at ease in the tub and have the water at a comfortable temperature. Begin bathing by wetting the coat all the way down to the skin. Massage in the shampoo, keeping it away from his face and eyes. Rinse him thoroughly, again avoiding the eyes and ears, as you don't want to get water into the ear canals. A thorough rinsing is important, as shampoo residue is drying and itchy to the dog. After rinsing, wrap him in a towel to absorb the initial moisture. You can finish drying with either a towel or a blow dryer on low heat, held at a safe distance from the dog. You should keep the dog indoors and away from drafts until he is completely dry.

NAIL CLIPPING

A Tibetan Mastiff's nails will need to be checked about once a month, though nails on dogs that walk regularly on hard surfaces will need less attention than those that spend most of their time on soft

---

THE MONTHLY GRIND

If your dog doesn't like the feeling of nail clippers or if you're not comfortable using them, you may wish to try an electric nail grinder. This tool has a small sandpaper disc on the end that rotates to grind the nails down. Some feel that using a grinder reduces the risk of cutting into the quick; this can be true if the tool is used properly. Usually you will be able to tell where the quick is before you get to it. A benefit of the grinder is that it creates a smooth finish on the nails so that there are no ragged edges.

Because the tool makes noise, your dog should be introduced to it before the actual grinding takes place. Turn it on and let your dog hear the noise; turn it off and let him inspect it with you holding it. Use the grinder gently, holding it firmly and progressing a little at a time until you reach the proper length. Look at the nail as you grind so that you do not go too short. Stop at any indication that you are nearing the quick. It will take a few sessions for both you and the puppy to get used to the grinder. Make sure that you don't let his hair get tangled in the grinder!

WATER SHORTAGE

Nothing can substitute for a good warm bath, but owners do have the option of giving their dogs "dry" baths. Pet shops sell excellent products, designed for spot-cleaning your dog. These dry shampoos are convenient for touch-up jobs when you don't have the time to bathe your dog in the traditional way or when using water is not a good idea (such as in cold weather or after whelping).

Muddy feet, messy behinds and smelly coats can be spot-cleaned and deodorized with a "wet-nap"-style cleaner. On those days when your dog insists on rolling in fresh goose droppings and there's no time for a bath, a spot bath can save the day. These pre-moistened wipes are also handy for other grooming needs like wiping faces, ears and eyes and freshening tails and behinds.

surfaces. For a dog of the Tibetan Mastiff's size, guillotine clippers are usually found to be the most efficient and easiest to handle, bearing in mind that some Tibetan Mastiffs object strongly to the procedure! To that end, your Tibetan Mastiff should be accustomed to having his nails trimmed at an early age since it will be part of your maintenance routine throughout his life. Not only does it look nicer, but long nails can scratch someone unintentionally. Also, a long nail has a better chance of ripping and bleeding, or causing the feet to spread. A good rule of thumb is that if you can hear your dog's nails clicking on the floor when he walks, his nails are too long.

Before you start cutting, make sure you can identify the "quick" in each nail. The quick is a blood vessel that runs through the center of each nail and grows rather close to the end. It will bleed if acciden-

tally cut, which will be quite painful for the dog as it contains nerve endings. Keep some type of clotting agent on hand, such as a styptic pencil or styptic powder (the type used for shaving). This will stop the bleeding quickly when applied to the end of the cut nail. Do not panic if you cut the quick, just stop the bleeding and talk soothingly to your dog. Once he has calmed down, move on to the next nail. It is better to clip a little at a time, particularly with black-nailed dogs.

Hold your pup steady as you begin trimming his nails; you do not want him to make any sudden movements or run away. Talk to him soothingly and stroke him as you clip. Holding his foot in your hand, simply take off the end of each nail in one quick clip. You can purchase nail clippers that are specially made for dogs; you can probably find them wherever you buy pet or grooming supplies.

EAR CLEANING

While keeping your dog's ears clean unfortunately will not cause him to "hear" your commands any better, it will protect him from ear infection and ear-mite infestation. In addition, a dog's ears are vulnerable to waxy build-up and to collecting foreign matter from the outdoors. Look in your dog's ears regularly to ensure that they look pink, clean and otherwise healthy. Even if they look fine, an odor in the ears signals a problem and means it's time to call the vet. If you see wax, brown droppings (a sign of ear mites), redness or any other abnormalities, contact your vet so that he can prescribe an appropriate medication.

A dog's ears should be cleaned regularly; once a month is suggested for the Tibetan Mastiff, and you can do this as part of one of your brushing sessions. Using a cotton ball or pad, and never probing into the ear canal, wipe the ear gently. You can use an ear-cleansing liquid or powder available from your vet or pet-supply store; alternatively, you might prefer to use homemade solutions with ingredients like white vinegar or hydrogen peroxide diluted with water. Ask your vet about home remedies before you attempt to concoct something on your own!

EYE CARE

During grooming sessions, pay extra attention to the condition of your dog's eyes. If the area around the eyes is soiled or if tear staining has occurred, there are various cleaning agents made especially for this purpose. Look at the dog's eyes to make sure no debris has entered; dogs who spend a lot of time outdoors are especially prone to this.

The signs of an eye infection are obvious: mucus, redness, puffiness, scabs or other signs of irritation. If your dog's eyes become infected, the vet will likely prescribe an antibiotic ointment for treatment. If you notice signs of more serious problems, such as opacities in the eye, which usually indicate cataracts, consult the vet at once. Taking time to pay attention to your dog's eyes will alert you in the early stages of any problem so that you can get your dog treatment as soon as possible. You could save your dog's sight!

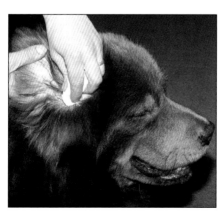

Clean your Tibetan Mastiff's ears with a cotton wipe and canine ear cleaner, usually available at your local pet-supply shop in liquid or powder form.

A CLEAN SMILE

Another essential part of grooming is brushing your dog's teeth and checking his overall oral condition. Studies show that around 80% of dogs experience dental problems by two years of age, and the percentage is higher in older dogs. Therefore it is highly likely that your dog will have trouble with his teeth and gums unless you are proactive with home dental care.

The most common dental problem in dogs is plaque build-up. If not treated, this causes gum disease, infection and resultant tooth loss. Bacteria from these infections spread throughout the body, affecting the vital organs. Do you need much more convincing to start brushing your dog's teeth? If so, take a good whiff of your dog's breath, and read on.

Fortunately, home dental care is rather easy and convenient for pet owners. Specially formulated canine toothpaste is easy to find. You should use one of these toothpastes, not a product for humans. Some doggie pastes are even available in flavors appealing to dogs. If your dog likes the flavor, he will tolerate the process better, making things much easier for you! Doggie toothbrushes come in different sizes and are designed to fit the contour of a canine mouth. Rubber fingertip brushes fit right on one of your

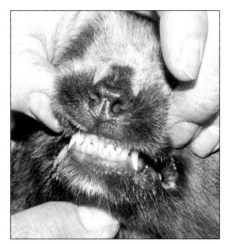

The puppy (temporary) teeth of an eight-week-old Tibetan Mastiff are indicative of the eventual bite characteristics of the mature dog. Brushing your dog's teeth should be started when he is a pup.

fingers and have rubber nodes to clean the teeth and massage the gums. This may be easier to handle, as it is akin to rubbing your dog's teeth with your finger.

As with other grooming tasks, accustom your Tibetan Mastiff pup to his dental care early on. Start gently, for a few minutes at a time, so that he gets used to the feel of the brush and to your handling his mouth. Offer praise and petting so that he looks at tooth-care time as a time when he gets extra love and attention. The routine should become second nature; he may not like it, but he should at least tolerate it.

Aside from brushing, offer dental toys to your dog and feed crunchy biscuits, which help to minimize plaque. When offered under supervision, uncooked beef knuckle bones are beneficial chew items for the Tibetan Mastiff. At your adult dog's yearly check-ups, the vet will likely perform a thorough tooth scraping as well as a complete check for any problems. Experienced owners often use a tooth-scraper to remove tartar, but you should only contemplate this if you have been shown exactly how to use one safely. It goes without saying that when cleaning teeth, you must be sure that both you and your dog trust each other completely. Proper care of your dog's teeth will ensure that you will enjoy your dog's smile for many years to come. The next time your dog goes to give you a hello kiss, you'll be glad you spent the time caring for his teeth.

THE OTHER END

Dogs sometime have troubles with their anal glands, which are sacs located beside the anal vent. These should empty when a dog has normal bowel movements; if they don't, they can become full or impacted, causing discomfort. Owners often are alarmed to see their dogs scooting across the floor, dragging their behinds behind; this is just a dog's attempt to empty the glands himself.

Some brave owners attempt to evacuate their dogs' anal glands themselves during grooming, but no one will tell you that this is a pleasant task! Thus, many owners prefer to make the trip to the vet to have the vet take care of the problem; owners whose dogs visit

a groomer can have this done by the groomer if he offers this as part of his services. Regardless, don't neglect the dog's other end in your home-care routine. Look for scooting, licking or other signs of discomfort "back there" to ascertain whether the anal glands need to be emptied. Often a higher fiber diet or adding flax seeds to the dog's food helps to prevent anal-gland problems.

IDENTIFICATION AND TRAVEL

ID FOR YOUR DOG

You love your Tibetan Mastiff and want to keep him safe. Of course you take every precaution to prevent his escaping from the yard or becoming lost or stolen. You have a sturdy high fence and you always keep your dog on lead when out and about in public places. If your dog is not properly identified, however, you are overlooking a major aspect of his safety. We hope to never be in a situation where our dog is missing, but we should practice prevention in the unfortunate case that this happens; identification greatly increases the chances of your dog's being returned to you.

There are several ways to identify your dog. First, the traditional dog tag should be a staple in your dog's wardrobe, attached to his everyday collar. Tags can be made of sturdy plastic and various metals and should

PET OR STRAY?
Besides the obvious benefit of providing your contact information to whoever finds your lost dog, an ID tag makes your dog more approachable and more likely to be recovered. A strange dog wandering the neighborhood without a collar and tags will look like a stray, while the collar and tags indicate that the dog is someone's pet. Even if the ID tags become detached from the collar, the collar alone will make a person more likely to pick up the dog.

include your contact information so that a person who finds the dog can get in touch with you right away to arrange his return. Many people today enjoy the wide range of decorative tags available, so have fun and create a tag to match your dog's personality. Of course, it is important that the tag stays on the collar, so have a secure "O" ring attachment; you also can explore the type of tag that slides right onto the collar.

In addition to the ID tag, which every dog should wear even if identified by another method, two other forms of identification have become popular: microchipping and tattooing. In microchipping, a tiny scannable chip is painlessly inserted under the dog's skin. The number is registered to you so that, if your lost dog turns up at a clinic or

shelter, the chip can be scanned to retrieve your contact information.

The advantage of the microchip is that it is a permanent form of ID, but there are some factors to consider. Several different companies make microchips, and not all are compatible with the others' scanning devices. It's best to find a company with a universal microchip that can be read by scanners made by other companies as well. It won't do any good to have the dog chipped if the information cannot be retrieved. Also, not every humane society, shelter and clinic is equipped with a scanner, although more and more facilities are equipping themselves. In fact, many shelters microchip dogs that they adopt out to new homes.

Because the microchip is not visible to the eye, the dog must wear a tag that states that he is microchipped so that whoever picks him up will know to have him scanned. This tag usually also includes the registry's phone number and the dog's microchip ID number. He of course also should have a tag with your contact information in case his chip information cannot be retrieved. Humane societies and veterinary clinics offer microchipping service, which is usually very affordable.

Though less popular than microchipping, tattooing is another permanent method of ID for dogs. Most vets perform this service, and

Show dogs are the most traveled of the canine set. It is not uncommon for show dogs to be driven long distances or to fly from coast to coast in large countries, such as the US, Canada and Australia.

there are also clinics that perform dog tattooing. This is also an affordable procedure and one that will not cause much discomfort for the dog. It is best to put the tattoo in a visible area, such as the ear, to deter theft. It is sad to say that there are cases of dogs' being stolen and sold to research laboratories, but such laboratories will not accept tattooed dogs.

To ensure that the tattoo is effective in aiding your dog's return to you, the tattoo number must be registered with a national organization. That way, when someone finds a tattooed dog, a phone call to the registry will quickly match the dog with his owner.

HIT THE ROAD

Car travel with your Tibetan Mastiff may be limited to necessity only, such as trips to the vet, or you may bring your dog along almost everywhere you go. This will depend much on your

individual dog and how he reacts to rides in the car. You can begin desensitizing your dog to car travel as a pup so that it's something that he's used to. Still, some dogs suffer from motion sickness. Your vet may prescribe a medication for this if trips in the car pose a problem for your dog. Young Tibetan Mastiff puppies sometimes are fed ginger snaps to soothe carsickness. At the very least, you will need to get him to the vet, so he will need to tolerate these trips with the least amount of hassle possible.

Start taking your pup on short trips, maybe just around the block to start. If he is fine with short trips, lengthen your rides a little at a time. Start to take him on your errands or just for drives around town. By this time it will be easy to tell whether your dog is a born traveler or would prefer staying at home when you are on the road.

Of course, safety is a concern for dogs in the car. First, he must travel securely, not left loose to roam about the car where he could be injured or distract the driver. A young pup can be held by a passenger initially but should soon graduate to a travel crate, which can be the same crate he uses in the home if your vehicle can accommodate his crate. Other options include a car harness (like a seat belt for dogs) and partitioning the back of the car with a gate made for this purpose.

Bring along what you will need

for the dog. He should wear his collar and ID tags, of course, and you should bring his leash, water (and food if a long trip) and clean-up materials for potty breaks and in case of motion sickness. Always keep your dog on his leash when you make stops, and never leave him alone in the car. Many a dog has died from the heat inside a parked car; this does not take much time at all. A dog left alone inside a car can also be a target for thieves.

BOARDING

Boarding a Tibetan Mastiff can be difficult as some boarding kennels may not accept the breed. Some facilities are just not set up for TMs. Boarding TMs is different in that they are not kept with other dogs and often are put in a separate area for cleaning and feeding.

You will need to start your search well in advance to find a kennel that will take your TM. Before you need to use such a service, check out the ones in your area. Make visits to see the facilities, meet the staff, discuss fees and available services and see whether this is a place where you think your dog will be happy. It is best to do your research in advance so that you're not stuck at the last minute, forced into making a rushed decision without knowing whether the kennel that you've chosen meets your standards. You also can check with your vet's office to see

whether they offer boarding for their clients or can recommend a good kennel in the area.

The kennel will need to see proof of your dog's health records and vaccinations so as not to spread illness from dog to dog. Your dog also will need proper identification. Owners usually experience some separation anxiety the first time they have to leave their dog in someone else's care, so it's reassuring to know that the kennel you choose is run by experienced, caring, true dog people. An alternative to boarding for TM owners is to leave their dog with people that the dog knows or to have someone that the dog knows come to the home to take care of the dog.

Your TM will be happy in a spacious yard, securely enclosed by a 6-foot-high fence, with precautions taken to prevent digging out.

TRAINING YOUR

TIBETAN MASTIFF

BASIC TRAINING PRINCIPLES: PUPPY VS. ADULT

There's a big difference between training an adult dog and training a young puppy. With a young puppy, everything is new! At eight to ten weeks of age, he will be experiencing many things, and he has nothing with which to compare these experiences. Up to this point, he has been with his dam and littermates, not one-on-one with people except in his interactions with his breeder and visitors to the litter.

When you first bring the puppy home, he is eager to please you. This means that he accepts doing things your way. During the next couple of months, he will absorb the basis of everything he needs to know for the rest of his life. This early age is even referred to as the "sponge" stage. After that, for the next 18 months, it's up to you to reinforce good manners by building on the foundation that you've established. Once your puppy is reliable in basic commands and behavior and has reached the appropriate age, you may gradually introduce him to some of the interesting sports, games and activities available to pet owners and their dogs.

Raising your puppy is a family affair. Each member of the family must know what rules to set forth for the puppy and how to use the same one-word commands to mean exactly the same thing every time. Even if yours is a large family, one person will soon be considered by the pup to be the leader, the

OUR CANINE KIDS

"Everything I learned about parenting, I learned from my dog." How often adults recognize that their parenting skills are mere extensions of the education they acquired while caring for their dogs. Many owners refer to their dogs as their "kids" and treat their canine companions like real members of the family. Surveys indicate that a majority of dog owners talk to their dogs regularly, celebrate their dogs' birthdays and purchase Christmas gifts for their dogs. Another survey shows that dog owners take their dogs to the veterinarian more frequently than they visit their own physicians.

alpha person in his pack, the "boss" who must be obeyed. Often that highly regarded person turns out to be the one who feeds the puppy. Food ranks very high on the puppy's list of important things! That's why your puppy is rewarded with small treats along with verbal praise when he responds to you correctly. As the puppy learns to do what you want him to do, the food rewards are gradually eliminated and only the praise remains. If you were to keep up with the food treats, you could have two problems on your hands—an obese dog and a beggar.

Training begins the minute your Tibetan Mastiff puppy steps through the doorway of your

home, so don't make the mistake of putting the puppy on the floor and telling him by your actions to "Go for it! Run wild!" Even if this is your first puppy, you must act as if you know what you're doing: be the boss. An uncertain pup may be terrified to move, while a bold one will be ready to take you at your word and start plotting to destroy the house. Before you collected your puppy, you decided where his own special place would be, and that's where to put him when you first arrive home. Give him a house tour after he has investigated his area and had a nap and a bathroom "pit stop."

A wonderful friendship can develop between a TM and a child who grow up together.

It's worth mentioning here that, if you've adopted an adult dog that is completely trained to your liking, lucky you! You're off the hook! However, if that dog spent his life up to this point in a kennel, or even in a good home

THE RIGHT START

The best advice for a potential dog owner is to start with the very best puppy that money can buy. Don't shop around for a bargain in the newspaper. You're buying a companion, not a used car or a secondhand appliance. The purchase price of the dog represents a very significant part of the investment, but this is indeed a very small sum compared to the expenses of maintaining the dog in good health. If you purchase a well-bred healthy and sound puppy, you will be starting right. An unhealthy puppy can cost you thousands of dollars in unnecessary veterinary expenses and, possibly, a fortune in heartbreak as well.

Breeder Susan Elworthy with four-month-old Linka. A trained dog is a wonderful companion.

Some new rules may be close to impossible for the dog to accept. After all, he's been successful so far by doing everything his way! (Patience again.) He may agree with your instruction for a few days and then slip back into his old ways, so you must be just as consistent and understanding in your teaching as you would be with a puppy. (More patience needed yet again!) Your dog has to learn to pay attention to your voice, your family, the daily routine, new smells, new sounds and, in some cases, even a new climate.

One of the most important things to find out about a newly adopted adult dog is his reaction to children (yours and others), strangers and your friends, and how he acts upon meeting other

but without any real training, be prepared to tackle the job ahead. An adult dog with no previous training cannot be blamed for not knowing what he was never taught. While the dog is trying to understand and learn your rules, at the same time he has to unlearn many of his previously self-taught habits and general view of the world.

Working with a professional trainer will speed up your progress with an adopted adult dog. You'll need patience, too.

CREATURES OF HABIT

Canine behaviorists and trainers aptly describe dogs as "creatures of habit," meaning that dogs respond to structure in their daily lives and welcome a routine. Do not interpret this to mean that dogs enjoy endless repetition in their training sessions. Dogs get bored just as humans do. Keep training sessions interesting and exciting. Vary the commands and the locations in which you practice. Give short breaks for play in between lessons. A bored student will never be the best performer in the class.

DAILY SCHEDULE

How many relief trips does your puppy need per day? A puppy up to the age of 14 weeks will need to go outside about 8 to 12 times per day! You will have to take the pup out any time he starts sniffing around the floor or turning in small circles, as well as after naps, meals, games and lessons or whenever he's released from his crate. Once the puppy is 14 to 22 weeks of age, he will require only 6 to 8 relief trips. At the ages of 22 to 32 weeks, the puppy will require about 5 to 7 trips. Adult dogs typically require 4 relief trips per day, in the morning, afternoon, evening and late at night.

HOUSE-TRAINING YOUR TIBETAN MASTIFF

The Tibetan Mastiff is by nature a very clean, intelligent animal who is relatively easy to house-train. Dogs are tactility-oriented when it comes to house-training. In other words, they respond to the surface on which they are given approval to eliminate. The choice is yours (the dog's version is in parentheses): The lawn (including the neighbors' lawns)? A bare patch of earth under a tree (where people like to sit and relax in the summertime)? Concrete steps or patio (all sidewalks, garages and basement floors)? The curbside (watch out for cars)? A small area of crushed

Ginger's look is unmistakable: "Can I have some privacy, please?"

dogs. If he was not socialized with dogs as a puppy, this could be a major problem. This does not mean that he's a "bad" dog, a vicious dog or an aggressive dog; rather, it means that he has no idea how to read another dog's body language. There's no way for him to tell whether the other dog is a friend or foe. Survival instinct takes over, telling him to attack first and ask questions later. This definitely calls for professional help and, even then, may not be a behavior that can be corrected 100% reliably (or even at all). If you have a puppy, this is why it is so very important to introduce your young puppy properly to other puppies and "dog-friendly" adult dogs.

stone in a corner of the yard (mine!)? The latter is the best choice if you can manage it, because it will remain strictly for the dog's use and is easy to keep clean.

You can start out with paper-training indoors and switch over to an outdoor surface as the puppy matures and gains control over his need to eliminate. For the naysayers, don't worry—this won't mean that the dog will soil on every piece of newspaper lying around the house. You are training him to go outside, remember? Starting out by paper-training often is the only choice for a city dog.

WHEN YOUR PUPPY'S "GOT TO GO"
Your puppy's need to relieve himself is seemingly non-stop, but signs of improvement will be seen each week. From 8–10 weeks old, the puppy will have to be taken outside every time he wakes up, about 10–15 minutes after every meal and after every period of play—all day long, from first thing in the morning until his bedtime! That's a total of ten or more trips per day to teach the puppy where it's okay to relieve himself. With that schedule in mind, you can see that house-training a young puppy is not a part-time job. It requires someone to be home all day.

If that seems overwhelming or impossible, do a little planning. For example, plan to pick up your puppy at the start of a vacation period. If you can't get home in the middle of the day, plan to hire a dog-sitter or ask a neighbor to come over to take the pup outside, feed him his lunch and then take him out again about ten or so minutes after he's eaten. Anyone who is coming to care for the dog when you're not home should be someone the pup is familiar with, and vice versa. Also make arrangements with that or another person to be your "emergency" contact if you have to stay late on the job. Remind yourself—repeatedly—that this hectic schedule improves as the puppy gets older.

TIDY BOY
Clean by nature, dogs do not like to soil their dens, which in effect are their crates or sleeping quarters. Unless not feeling well, dogs will not defecate or urinate in their crates. Crate training capitalizes on the dog's natural desire to keep his den clean. Be conscientious about giving the puppy as many opportunities to relieve himself outdoors as possible. Reward the puppy for correct behavior. Praise him and pat him whenever he "goes" in the correct location. Even the tidiest of puppies can have potty accidents, so be patient and dedicate more energy to helping your puppy achieve a clean lifestyle.

HOME WITHIN A HOME

Your Tibetan Mastiff puppy needs to be confined to one secure, puppy-proof area when no one is able to watch his every move. Generally, the kitchen is the place of choice because the floor is washable. Likewise, it's a busy family area that will accustom the pup to a variety of noises, everything from pots and pans to the telephone, blender and dishwasher. He will also be enchanted by the smell of your cooking (and will never be critical when you burn something). A sturdy exercise pen (also called an "ex-pen," a puppy version of a playpen) within the room of choice is a good means of confinement for a young pup as long as he cannot jump or climb out. He can see out and has a certain amount of space in which to run about, but he is safe from dangerous things like electrical cords, heating units, trash baskets or open kitchen-supply cabinets. Place the pen where the puppy will not get a blast of heat or air conditioning.

In the pen, you can put a few toys, his bed (which can be his crate if the dimensions of pen and crate are compatible) and a few layers of newspaper in one small corner, just in case. A water bowl can be hung at a convenient height on the side of the ex-pen so it won't become a splashing pool for an innovative puppy. His

> ### EXTRA! EXTRA!
> The headlines read: "Puppy Piddles Here!" Breeders commonly use newspapers to line their whelping pens, so puppies learn to associate newspapers with relieving themselves. Do not use newspapers to line your pup's crate, as this will signal to your puppy that it is OK to urinate in his crate. If you choose to paper-train your puppy, you will layer newspapers on a section of the floor near the door he uses to go outside. You should encourage the puppy to use the papers to relieve himself, and bring him there whenever you see him getting ready to go. Little by little, you will reduce the size of the newspaper-covered area so that the puppy will learn to relieve himself "on the other side of the door."

food dish can go on the floor, next to but not under the water bowl.

Crates are something that pet owners are at last getting used to for their dogs. Wild or domestic canines have always preferred to sleep in den-like safe spots, and that is exactly what the crate provides. How often have you seen adult dogs that choose to sleep under a table or chair even though they have full run of the house? It's the den connection.

In your "happy" voice, use the word "Crate" every time you put the pup into his den. If he's new to a crate, toss in a small biscuit for him to chase the first few times. At night, after he's been outside, he should sleep in his crate. The crate may be kept in his designated area at night or, if you want to be sure to hear those wake-up yips in the morning, put the crate in a corner of your bedroom. However, don't make any response whatsoever to whining or crying. If he's completely ignored, he'll settle down and get to sleep.

Good bedding for a young puppy is an old folded bath towel or an old blanket, something that is easily washable and disposable if necessary ("accidents" will happen!). Never put newspaper in the puppy's crate. Also those old ideas about adding a clock to replace his mother's heartbeat or a hot-water bottle to replace her warmth, are just that—old ideas. The clock could drive the puppy nuts, and the hot-water bottle

This dog knows the routine and his signal is clear: "It's time to go out."

TEACHER'S PET

Dogs are individuals, not robots, with many traits basic to their breed. Some, bred to work alone, are independent thinkers; others rely on you to call the shots. If you have enrolled in a training class, your instructor can offer alternative methods of training based on your individual dog's instincts and personality. You may benefit from using a different type of collar or switching to a class with different kinds of dogs.

could end up as a very soggy waterbed! An extremely good breeder would have introduced your puppy to the crate by letting two pups sleep together for a couple of nights, followed by several nights alone. How thankful you will be if you found that breeder!

Safe toys in the pup's crate or area will keep him occupied, but monitor their condition closely. Discard any toys that show signs of being chewed to bits. Squeaky parts, bits of stuffing or plastic or any other small pieces can cause intestinal blockage or possibly choking if swallowed.

PROGRESSING WITH POTTY-TRAINING
After you've taken your puppy out and he has relieved himself in the area you've selected, he can have some free time with the family as long as there is

someone responsible for watching him. That doesn't mean just someone in the same room who is watching TV or busy on the computer, but one person who is doing nothing other than keeping an eye on the pup, playing with him on the floor and helping him understand his position in the pack.

This first taste of freedom will let you begin to set the house rules. If you don't want the dog on the furniture, now is the time to prevent his first attempts to jump up onto the couch. The word to use in this case is "Off," not "Down." "Down" is the word you will use to teach the down position, which is something entirely different.

Most corrections at this stage come in the form of simply distracting the puppy. Instead of telling him "No" for "Don't chew the carpet," distract the chomping puppy with a toy and he'll forget about the carpet.

As you are playing with the pup, do not forget to watch him closely and pay attention to his body language. Whenever you see him begin to circle or sniff, take the puppy outside to relieve himself. If you are paper-training, put him back into his confined area on the newspapers. In either case, praise him as he eliminates while he actually is in the act of relieving himself. Three seconds after he has finished is too late!

You'll be praising him for running toward you, picking up a toy or whatever he may be doing at that moment, and that's not what you want to be praising him for. Timing is a vital tool in all dog training. Use it!

If you decided to start out with paper-training, remove soiled newspapers immediately and replace them with clean ones. You may want to take a small piece of soiled paper and place it in the middle of the new clean papers, as the scent will attract him to that spot when it's time to go again. That scent attraction is why it's so important to clean up any messes made in the house by using a product specially made to eliminate the odor of dog urine and droppings.

Like all young puppies, ten-week-old Coqo is a blank slate, waiting to learn all you can teach her.

Regular household cleansers won't do the trick. Pet shops sell the best pet deodorizers. Invest in the largest container you can find.

Scent attraction eventually will lead your pup to his chosen spot outdoors; this is the basis of outdoor training. When you take your puppy outside to relieve himself, use a one-word command such as "Outside" or "Go-potty" (that's one word to the puppy!) as you attach his leash. Then lead him to his spot. Now comes the hard part—hard for you, that is. Just stand there until he urinates and defecates. Move him a few feet in one direction or another if he's just sitting there looking at you, but remember that this is neither playtime nor time for a walk. This is strictly a business trip. Then, as he circles and squats (remember your timing!), give him a quiet "Good dog" as praise. If you start to jump for joy, ecstatic over his performance, he'll do one of two things: either he will stop mid-stream, as it were, or he'll do it again for you—in the house—and expect you to be just as delighted.

Give him five minutes or so and, if he doesn't go in that time, take him back indoors to his confined area and try again in another ten minutes, or immediately if you see him sniffing and circling. By careful observation, you'll soon work out a successful schedule.

BASIC PRINCIPLES OF DOG TRAINING
1. Start training early. A young puppy is ready, willing and able.
2. Timing is your all-important tool. Praise at the exact time that the dog responds correctly. Pay close attention.
3. Patience is almost as important as timing!
4. Repeat! The same word has to mean the same thing every time.
5. In the beginning, praise all correct behavior verbally, along with treats and petting.

Accidents, by the way, are just that—accidents. Clean them up quickly and thoroughly, without comment, after the puppy has been taken outside to finish his business and then put back into his area or crate. If you witness an accident in progress, say "No!" in a stern voice and get the pup outdoors immediately. No punishment is needed. You and your puppy are just learning each other's language, and sometimes it's easy to miss a puppy's message. Chalk it up to experience and watch more closely from now on.

KEEPING THE PACK ORDERLY
Discipline is a form of training that brings order to life. For example, military discipline is what allows the soldiers in an

army to work as one. Discipline is a form of teaching and, in dogs, is the basis of how the successful pack operates. Each member knows his place in the pack and all respect the leader, or alpha dog. It is essential for your puppy that you establish this type of relationship, with you as the alpha, or leader. It is a form of social coexistence that all canines recognize and accept. Discipline, therefore, is never to be confused with punishment. When you teach your puppy how you want him to behave, and he behaves properly and you praise him for it, you are disciplining him with a form of positive reinforcement.

For a dog, rewards come in the form of praise, a smile, a cheerful tone of voice, a few friendly pats or a rub of the ears. Rewards are also small food treats. Obviously, that does not mean bits of regular dog food. Instead, treats are very small bits of special things like cheese or

pieces of soft dog treats. The idea is to reward the dog with something very small that he can taste and swallow, providing instant positive reinforcement. If he has to take time to chew the treat, by the time he is finished he will have forgotten what he did to earn it!

Your puppy should never be physically punished. The displeasure shown on your face and in your voice is sufficient to signal to the pup that he has done something wrong. He wants to please everyone higher up on the social ladder, especially his leader, so a scowl and harsh voice will take care of the error. Growling out the word "Shame!" when the pup is caught in the act of doing something wrong is better than the repetitive "No."

You are the leader of your Tibetan Mastiff's pack, and it is up to you to establish a bond of respect and trust so that he will live by your rules.

SHOULD WE ENROLL?

Puppy kindergarten classes are a must for your Tibetan Mastiff. In these classes, puppies of all sizes learn basic lessons while getting the opportunity to meet and greet each other; it's as much about socialization as it is about good manners. What you learn in class you can practice at home. And if you goof up in practice, you'll get help in the next session.

Some dogs hear "No" so often that they begin to think it's their name! By the way, do not use the dog's name when you're correcting him. His name is reserved to get his attention for something pleasant about to take place.

There are punishments that have nothing to do with you. For example, your dog may think that chasing cats is one reason for his existence. You can try to stop it as much as you like but without success, because it's such fun for the dog. But one good hissing, spitting swipe of a cat's claws across the dog's nose will put an end to the game forever. Intervene only when your dog's eyeball is seriously at risk. Cat scratches can cause permanent damage to an innocent but annoying puppy.

SMILE WHEN YOU ORDER ME AROUND!

While trainers recommend practicing with your dog every day, it's perfectly acceptable to take a "mental health day" off. It's better not to train the dog on days when you're in a sour mood. Your bad attitude or lack of interest will be sensed by your dog, and he will respond accordingly. Studies show that dogs are well tuned in to their humans' emotions. Be conscious of how you use your voice when talking to your dog. Raising your voice or shouting will only erode your dog's trust in you as his trainer and master.

PUPPY KINDERGARTEN

COLLAR AND LEASH

Before you begin your Tibetan Mastiff puppy's education, he must be used to his collar and leash. Choose a collar for your puppy that is secure, but not heavy or bulky. He won't enjoy training if he's uncomfortable. A rolled nylon or leather collar is fine for everyday wear and for initial puppy training. For adult Tibetan Mastiffs, the recommended training collar is the rolled nylon or metal snake chain choke collar. With unruly large puppies or adults, a choke prong collar can be very effective when used properly.

A lightweight 6-foot woven cotton or nylon training leash is preferred by most trainers because it is easy to fold up in your hand and comfortable to hold because there is a certain amount of give to it. There are lessons where the dog will start off 6 feet away from you at the end of the leash. The leash used to take the puppy outside to relieve himself is shorter because you don't want him to roam away from his area. The shorter leash will also be the one to use when you walk the puppy. A heavy-duty retractable lead made for large/giant breeds can be a safe way to exercise your dog in open areas like a park or field.

CANINE DEVELOPMENT SCHEDULE

It is important to understand how and at what age a puppy develops into adulthood.
If you are a puppy owner, consult this Canine Development Schedule to
determine the stage of development your puppy is currently experiencing.
This knowledge will help you as you work with the puppy in the weeks and months ahead.

PERIOD	AGE	CHARACTERISTICS
FIRST TO THIRD	BIRTH TO SEVEN WEEKS	Puppy needs food, sleep and warmth and responds to simple and gentle touching. Needs mother for security and disciplining. Needs littermates for learning and interacting with other dogs. Pup learns to function within a pack and learns pack order of dominance. Begin socializing pup with adults and children for short periods. Pup begins to become aware of his environment.
FOURTH	EIGHT TO TWELVE WEEKS	Brain is fully developed. Pup needs socializing with outside world. Remove from mother and littermates. Needs to change from canine pack to human pack. Human dominance necessary. Fear period occurs between 8 and 12 weeks. Avoid fright and pain.
FIFTH	THIRTEEN TO SIXTEEN WEEKS	Training and formal obedience should begin at home until pup is fully vaccinated after four months. Period will pass easily if you remember this is pup's change-to-adolescence time. Be firm and fair. Flight instinct prominent. Permissiveness and over-disciplining can do permanent damage. Praise for good behavior.
JUVENILE	FOUR TO EIGHT MONTHS	Less association with other dogs, more with people, places, situations. Another fear period about 7 to 8 months of age. It passes quickly, but be cautious of fright and pain. Sexual maturity reached. Dominant traits established. Dog should understand sit, down, come and stay by now.

NOTE: THESE ARE APPROXIMATE TIME FRAMES. ALLOW FOR INDIVIDUAL DIFFERENCES IN PUPPIES.

If you've been wise enough to enroll in a puppy kindergarten training class, suggestions will be made as to the best collar and leash for your young puppy. I say "wise" because your puppy will be in a class with puppies in his age range (up to five months old) of all breeds and sizes. It's the perfect way for him to learn the right way (and the wrong way) to interact with other dogs as well as their people. You cannot teach your puppy how to interpret another dog's sign language. For a first-time puppy owner, these socialization classes are invaluable. For experienced dog owners, they are a real boon to further training.

TRAINING YOUR TM PUPPY

The Tibetan Mastiff is one of the most intelligent and most stubborn breeds. Think of a strong-willed child. Most of the TM's guarding behavior is natural, instinctive and realized in his own spacious yard. Understand this, and you will have better success training your TM puppy. Tibetan Mastiffs are independent, cat-like thinkers with whom you have to strike a treaty. They respond best to owner-training at home or in puppy classes, not to being sent off somewhere to be trained. Simple commands, patience, praise and motivating with a favorite treat get the best results.

ATTENTION

You've been using the dog's name since the minute you collected him from the breeder, so you should be able to get his attention by saying his name—with a big smile and in an excited tone of voice. His response will be the puppy equivalent of "Here I am! What are we going to do?" Your immediate response (if you haven't guessed by now) is "Good dog." Rewarding him at the moment he pays attention to you teaches him the proper way to respond when he hears his name.

BASIC CANINE EXERCISES

THE SIT EXERCISE

There are several ways to teach the puppy to sit. The first one is to catch him whenever he is about to sit and, as his backside nears the floor, say "Sit, good dog!" That's positive reinforcement and, if your timing is sharp, he will learn that what he's doing at that second is connected to your saying "Sit" and that you think he's clever for doing it!

Another method is to start with the puppy on his leash in front of you. Show him a treat in the palm of your right hand. Bring your hand up under his nose and, almost in slow motion, move your hand up and back so his nose goes up in the air and his head tilts back as he follows the treat in your hand. At that point, he will have to either sit or fall over, so as his back legs buckle under, say "Sit, good dog," and then give him the treat and lots of praise. You may have to begin with your hand lightly running up his chest, actually lifting his chin up until he sits. Some (usually older) dogs require gentle pressure on their hindquarters with the left hand, in which case the dog should be on your left side. Puppies generally do not appreciate this physical dominance.

After a few times, you should be able to show the dog a treat in the open palm of your hand, raise your hand waist-high as you say "Sit" and have him sit, thereby teaching him two things at the same time. Both the verbal command and the motion of the hand are signals for the sit. Your puppy is watching you almost more than he is listening to you, so what you do is just as important as what you say.

Don't save any of these drills only for training sessions. Use them as much as possible at odd times during a normal day. The dog should always sit before being given his food dish. He should sit to let you go through a doorway first, when the doorbell rings or when you stop to speak to someone on the street.

THE DOWN EXERCISE

Before beginning to teach the down command, you must

consider how the dog feels about this exercise. To him, "down" is a submissive position. Being flat on the floor with you standing over him is not his idea of fun. It's up to you to let him know that, while it may not be fun, the reward of your approval is worth his effort.

Start with the puppy on your left side in a sit position. Hold the leash right above his collar in your left hand. Have an extra-

Timo quickly learned that a "high five" would earn him a biscuit.

special treat, such as a small piece of cooked chicken or hot dog, in your right hand. Place it at the end of the pup's nose and steadily move your hand down and forward along the ground. Hold the leash to prevent a sudden lunge for the food. As the puppy goes into the down position, say "Down" very gently.

The difficulty with this exercise is twofold: it's both the submissive aspect and the fact that most people say the word "Down" as if they were drill sergeants in charge of recruits! So issue the command sweetly, give him the treat and have the pup maintain the down position for several seconds. If he tries to get up immediately, place your hands on his shoulders and press down gently, giving him a very quiet "Good dog." As you progress with this lesson, increase the "down time" until he will hold it

Relaxing in the down position is the beautiful Tibetan import Cola.

> **TIPS FOR TRAINING AND SAFETY**
> 1. Whether on or off leash, practice only in a fenced area.
> 2. Remove the training collar when the training session is over.
> 3. Use caution when breaking up a dogfight.
> 4. "Come," "Leave it" and "Wait" are safety commands.
> 5. The dog belongs in a crate or behind a barrier when riding in the car.
> 6. Don't ignore the dog's first sign of aggression. Aggression only gets worse, so take it seriously.
> 7. Supervise your dog with children.
> 8. Pay attention to what the dog is chewing.
> 9. Keep the vet's number near your phone.
> 10. "Okay" is a useful release command.

until you say "Okay" (his cue for release). Practice this one in the house at various times throughout the day.

By increasing the length of time during which the dog must maintain the down position, you'll find many uses for it. For example, he can lie at your feet in the vet's office or anywhere that both of you have to wait, when you are on the phone, while the family is eating and so forth. If you progress to training for competitive obedience, he'll already be all set for the exercise called the "long down."

THE STAY EXERCISE

You can teach your Tibetan Mastiff to stay in the sit, down and stand positions. To teach the sit/stay, have the dog sit on your left side. Hold the leash at waist level in your left hand and let the dog know that you have a treat in your closed right hand. Step forward on your right foot as you say "Stay." Immediately turn and stand directly in front of the dog, keeping your right hand up high so he'll keep his eye on the treat hand and maintain the sit position for a count of five. Return to your original position and offer the reward.

Increase the length of the sit/stay each time until the dog can hold it for at least 30 seconds without moving. After about a week of success, move out on your right foot and take two steps before turning to face the dog. Give the "Stay" hand signal (left palm held up, facing the dog's head) as you leave. He gets the treat when you return and he holds the sit/stay. Increase the distance that you walk away from him before turning until you reach the length of your training leash. But don't rush it! Go back to the beginning if he moves before he should. No matter what the lesson, never be upset by having to back up for a few days. The repetition and practice are what will make your dog reliable in these commands. It won't do

> ## COME AND GET IT!
> The come command is your dog's safety signal. Until he is 99% perfect in responding, don't use the come command if you cannot enforce it. Practice on leash with treats or squeakers, or whenever the dog is running to you. Never call him to come to you if he is to be corrected for a misdemeanor. Reward the dog with a treat and happy praise whenever he comes to you.

any good to move on to something more difficult if the command is not mastered at the easier levels. Above all, even if you do get frustrated, never let your puppy know! Always keep a positive, upbeat attitude during training, which will transmit to your dog for positive results.

The down/stay is taught in the same way once the dog is completely reliable and steady with the down command. Again, don't rush it. With the dog in the down position on your left side,

Teaching the TM the down/stay command can be challenging. Here, Andorg behaves because he wants to!

step out on your right foot as you say "Stay." Return by walking around in back of the dog and into your original position. While you are training, it's okay to murmur something like "Hold on" to encourage him to stay put. When the dog will stay without moving when you are at a distance of 3 or 4 feet, begin to increase the length of time before you return. Be sure he holds the down on your return until you say "Okay." At that point, he gets his treat—just so he'll remember for next time that it's not over until it's over.

THE COME EXERCISE

No command is more important to the safety of your Tibetan Mastiff than "Come." It is what you should say every single time you see the puppy running toward you: "Murphy, come! Good dog." During playtime, run a few feet away from the puppy and turn and tell him to "Come"

Tibetan Mastiffs do best in the company of canine companions, especially other TMs.

as he is already running to you. You can go so far as to teach your puppy two things at once if you squat down and hold out your arms. As the pup gets close to you and you're saying "Good dog," bring your right arm in about waist high. Now he's also learning the hand signal, an excellent device should you be on the phone when you need to get him to come to you! You'll also both be one step ahead when you enter obedience classes.

When the puppy responds to your well-timed "Come," try it with the puppy on the training leash. This time, catch him off guard, while he's sniffing a leaf or watching a bird: "Murphy, come!" You may have to pause for a split second after his name to be sure you have his attention. If the puppy shows any sign of confusion, give the leash a mild jerk and take a couple of steps backward. Do not repeat the command. In this case, you should say "Good come" as he reaches you.

That's an important rule of training. Each command word is given just once. Anything more is nagging. You'll also notice that all commands are one word only. Even when they are actually two words, you say them as one.

Never call the dog to come to you—with or without his name—if you are angry or intend to correct him for some misbehavior.

When correcting the pup, you go to him. Your dog must always connect "Come" with something pleasant and with your approval; then you can rely on his response.

Puppies, like children, have notoriously short attention spans, so don't overdo it with any of the training. Keep each lesson short. Break it up with a quick run around the yard or a ball toss, repeat the lesson and quit as soon as the pup gets it right. That way, you will always end with a "Good dog."

Life isn't perfect and neither are puppies. A time will come, often around ten months of age, when he'll become "selectively deaf" or choose to "forget" his name. He may respond by wagging his tail (and even seeming to smile at you) with a look that says "Make me!" Laugh, throw his favorite toy and skip the lesson you had planned. Pups will be pups!

THE HEEL EXERCISE

The second most important command to teach, after the come, is the heel. When you are walking your growing puppy, you need to be in control. Besides, it looks terrible to be pulled and yanked down the street, and it's not much fun either—imagine trying to walk an out-of-control dog with the size and strength of the adult TM. Your eight-to ten-

> **LET'S GO!**
> Many people use "Let's go" instead of "Heel" when teaching their dogs to behave on lead. It sounds more like fun! When beginning to teach the heel, whatever command you use, always step off on your left foot. That's the one next to the dog, who is on your left side, in case you've forgotten. Keep a loose leash. When the dog pulls ahead, stop, bring him back and begin again. Use treats to guide him around turns.

week-old puppy will probably follow you everywhere, but that's his natural instinct, not your control over the situation. However, any time he does follow you, you can say "Heel" and be ahead of the game, as he will learn to associate this command with the action of following you before you even begin teaching him to heel.

There is a very precise, almost military, procedure for teaching your dog to heel. As with all other obedience training, begin with the dog on your left side. He will be in a very nice sit and you will have the training leash across your chest. Hold the loop and folded leash in your right hand. Pick up the slack leash above the dog in your left hand and hold it loosely at your side. Step out on your left foot as you say "Heel." If the puppy does not move, give a gentle tug or pat your left leg to get him started. If he surges ahead of you, stop and pull him back gently until he is at your side. Tell him to sit and begin again.

Walk a few steps and stop while the puppy is correctly beside you. Tell him to sit and give mild verbal praise. (More enthusiastic praise will encourage him to think the lesson is over.) Repeat the lesson, increasing the number of steps you take only as long as the dog is heeling nicely beside you. When you end the lesson, have him hold the sit, then give him the "Okay" to let him know that this is the end of the lesson. Praise him so that he knows he did a good job.

The cure for excessive pulling (a common problem) is to stop when the dog is no more than 2 or 3 feet ahead of you. Guide him back into position and begin again. With a really determined puller, try switching to a head collar. When used properly, this

will automatically turn the pup's head toward you so you can bring him back easily to the heel position. Give quiet, reassuring praise every time the leash goes slack and he's staying with you.

Staying and heeling can take a lot out of a dog, so provide playtime and free-running exercise in the fenced yard to shake off the stress when the lessons are over. You don't want him to associate training with all work and no fun.

TAPERING OFF TIDBITS
Your dog has been watching you—and the hand that treats— throughout all of his lessons, and now it's time to break the treat habit. Begin by giving him treats at the end of each lesson only. Then start to give a treat after the end of only some of the lessons. At the end of every lesson, as well as during the lessons, be consistent with the praise. Your pup now doesn't know whether he'll get a treat or not, but he should keep performing well just in case! Finally, you will stop giving treat rewards entirely. Save them for something brand-new that you want to teach him. Keep up the praise and you'll always have a "good dog."

OBEDIENCE CLASSES
Although it is not easy to train a Tibetan Mastiff, it is not impossible. Patience, persever-

Although TMs are not seen too often in agility, it is not beyond their capability. Here an owner guides his TM through the weave-pole obstacle.

ance and consistency are of paramount importance when training your Tibetan Mastiff. It is important to work with an obedience trainer who has a good under- standing of the breed's temper- ament. It is a good idea to interview instruc- tors and/or watch a few of their classes prior to starting any training program. A good instructor will meet with you and your dog for an individual assessment prior to starting a training program with you.

The advantages of an obedience class are that your dog will have to learn amid the distractions of other people and dogs and that your mistakes will be quickly corrected by the trainer. Teaching your dog along with a qualified instructor and other handlers who may have more dog experience than you is another plus of the class environment. The instructor and other handlers can help you to find the most efficient way of teaching your dog a command or exercise. It's often easier to learn from other people's mistakes than your own. You will also

Although the Tibetan Mastiff is a heavy dog, standing 2 feet or more at the shoulder, he is still an agile and active dog.

learn all of the requirements for competitive obedience trials, in which you can earn titles, which are fun for many dogs. Obedience classes build the foundation needed for many other canine activities (in which we humans are allowed to participate, too!).

This group of TMs and their owners are participating in an informal match show. Matches are ideal for socializing your TM and getting acquainted with show procedure.

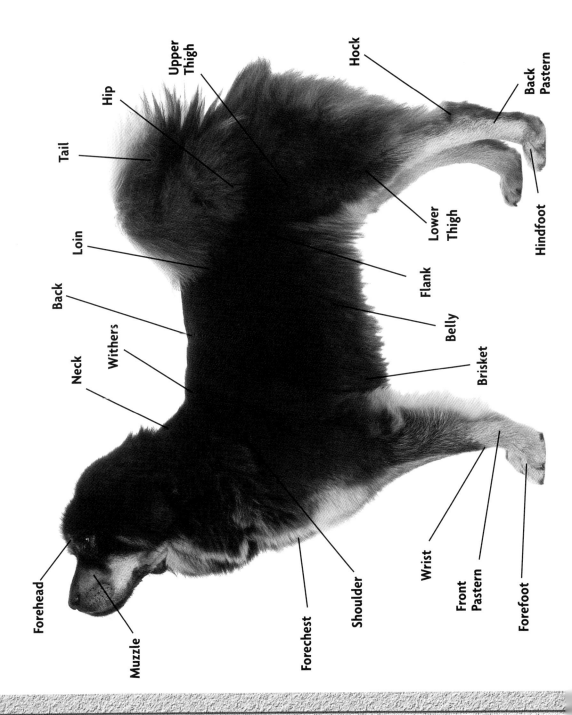

PHYSICAL STRUCTURE OF THE TIBETAN MASTIFF

Upper Thigh

Hock

Back Pastern

Hip

Tail

Lower Thigh

Hindfoot

Loin

Flank

Back

Belly

Withers

Brisket

Neck

Wrist

Forehead

Front Pastern

Muzzle

Forechest

Shoulder

Forefoot

TIBETAN MASTIFF

By Lowell Ackerman DVM, DACVD

HEALTHCARE FOR A LIFETIME
When you own a dog, you become his healthcare advocate over his entire lifespan, as well as being the one to shoulder the financial burden of such care. Accordingly, it is worthwhile to focus on prevention rather than treatment, as you and your pet will both be happier.

Of course, the best place to have begun your program of preventive healthcare is with the initial purchase or adoption of your dog. There is no way of guaranteeing that your new furry friend is free of medical problems, but there are some things you can do to improve your odds. You certainly should have done adequate research into the Tibetan Mastiff and have selected your puppy carefully rather than buying on impulse. Health issues aside, a large number of pet abandonment and relinquishment cases arise from a mismatch between pet needs and owner expectations. This is entirely preventable with appropriate planning and finding a good breeder.

Regarding healthcare issues specifically, it is very difficult to make blanket statements about where to acquire a problem-free pet, but, again, a reputable breeder is your best bet. In an ideal situation you have the opportunity to see both parents, get references from other owners of the breeder's pups and see genetic-testing documentation for several generations of the litter's ancestors. At the very least, you must thoroughly investigate the Tibetan Mastiff and the problems inherent in that breed, as well as the genetic testing available to screen for those problems. Genetic testing offers some important benefits but is available for only a few disorders in a relatively small number of breeds and is not available for some of the most common genetic diseases, such as hip dysplasia, cataracts, epilepsy, cardiomy-opathy, etc. This area of research is indeed exciting and increas-ingly important, and advances will continue to be made each year. In fact, recent research has shown that there is an equivalent dog gene for 75% of known human genes, so research done in

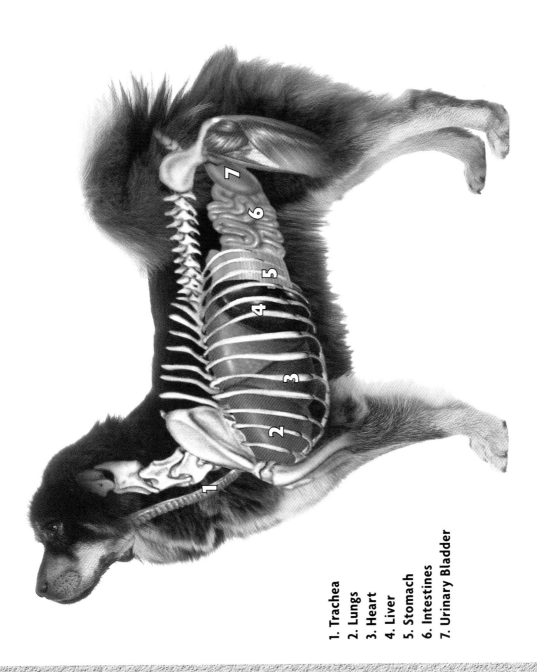

1. Trachea
2. Lungs
3. Heart
4. Liver
5. Stomach
6. Intestines
7. Urinary Bladder

INTERNAL ORGANS OF THE TIBETAN MASTIFF

either species is likely to benefit the other.

We've also discussed that evaluating the behavioral nature of your Tibetan Mastiff and that of his immediate family members is an important part of the selection process that cannot be underestimated or overemphasized. It is sometimes difficult to evaluate temperament in puppies because certain behavioral tendencies, such as some forms of aggression, may not be immediately evident. More dogs are euthanized each year for behavioral reasons than for all medical conditions combined, so it is critical to take temperament issues seriously. Start with a well-balanced, friendly companion and put the time and effort into proper socialization, and you will both be rewarded with a valued relationship for the life of the dog.

Assuming that you have started off with a pup from healthy, sound stock, you then become responsible for helping your veterinarian keep your pet healthy. Some crucial things happen before you even bring your puppy home. Parasite control typically begins at two weeks of age, and vaccinations typically begin at six to eight weeks of age. A pre-pubertal evaluation is typically scheduled for about six months of age. At this time, a dental evaluation is

done (since the adult teeth are now in), heartworm prevention is started and neutering or spaying is most commonly done.

It is critical to commence regular dental care at home if you have not already done so. It may not sound very important, but most dogs have active periodontal disease by four years of age if

DENTAL WARNING SIGNS

A veterinary dental exam is necessary if you notice one or any combination of the following in your dog:
• Broken, loose or missing teeth
• Loss of appetite (which could be due to mouth pain or illness caused by infection)
• Gum abnormalities, including redness, swelling and bleeding
• Drooling, with or without blood
• Yellowing of the teeth or gumline, indicating tartar
• Bad breath

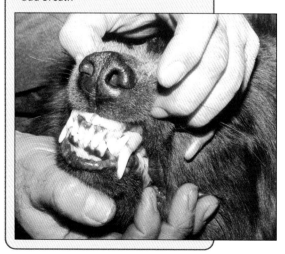

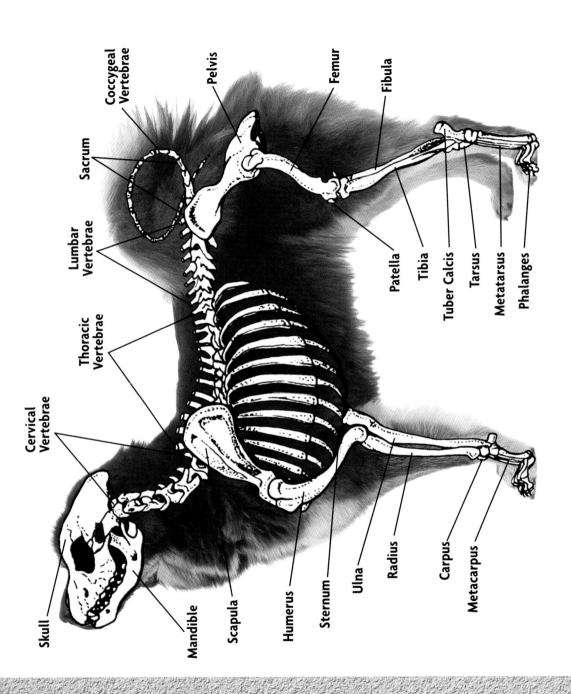

SKELETAL STRUCTURE OF THE TIBETAN MASTIFF

they don't have their teeth cleaned regularly at home, not just at their veterinary exams. Dental problems lead to more than just bad "doggy breath." Gum disease can have very serious medical consequences. If you start brushing your dog's teeth and using antiseptic rinses from a young age, your dog will be accustomed to it and will not resist. The results will be healthy dentition, which your pet will need to enjoy a long, healthy life.

The Tibetan Mastiff is slow to mature, with both males and females not reaching maturity until three to four years old. Even individual dogs within each breed have different healthcare requirements, so work with your veterinarian to determine what will be needed and what your role should be. This doctor-client relationship is important, because as vaccination guidelines change, there may not be an annual "vaccine visit" scheduled. You must make sure that you see your veterinarian at least annually, even if no vaccines are due, because this is the best opportunity to coordinate healthcare activities and to make sure that no medical issues creep by unaddressed.

At around seven years of age, your Tibetan Mastiff will be considered a "senior" and likely requires some special care. In general, if you've been taking

> **TMCA HEALTH DATABASE**
> The Tibetan Mastiff Club of America, in interest of promoting the wellness of the breed, is sponsoring an online survey to help determine the prevalence of diseases and health conditions within the Tibetan Mastiff community. This survey is not limited to TMCA members; any owner can enter his Tibetan Mastiff. The health survey is ongoing and the information collected will be used to create a health database for the breed. Responses will be kept confidential. Owners will be able to access and update their dogs' information at any time. The survey can be found at the club's website: www.tmcamerica.org.

great care of your canine companion throughout his formative and adult years, the transition to senior status should be a smooth one. Age is not a disease, and as long as everything is functioning as it should, there is no reason why most of late adulthood should not be rewarding for both you and your pet. This is especially true if you have tended to the details, such as regular veterinary visits, proper dental care, excellent nutrition and management of bone and joint issues.

At this stage in your Tibetan Mastiff's life, your veterinarian should want to schedule visits twice yearly, instead of once, to run some laboratory screenings, electrocardiograms and the like, and perhaps to change the diet to something more digestible. Catching problems early is the best way to manage them effectively. Treating the early stages of heart disease is so much easier than trying to intervene when there is more significant damage to the heart muscle. Similarly, managing the beginning of kidney problems is fairly routine if there is no significant kidney damage. Other problems, like cognitive dysfunction (similar to senility and Alzheimer's disease), cancer, diabetes and arthritis, are more common in older dogs, but all can be treated to help the dog live as many happy, comfortable years as possible. Just as in people, medical management is more effective (and less expensive) when you catch things early.

SELECTING A VETERINARIAN
There is probably no more important decision that you will make regarding your pet's healthcare than the selection of his doctor. Your pet's veterinarian will be a pediatrician, family-practice physician and gerontologist, depending on the dog's life stage, and will be the individual who makes recommendations regarding issues such as when specialists need to be consulted, when diagnostic testing and/or

therapeutic intervention is needed and when you will need to seek outside emergency and critical-care services. Your vet will act as your advocate and liaison throughout these processes.

Everyone has his own idea about what to look for in a vet, an individual who will play a big role in his dog's (and, of course, his own) life for many years to come. For some, it is the compassionate caregiver with whom they hope to develop a professional relationship to span the lives of their dogs and even their future pets. For others, they are seeking a clinician with keen diagnostic and therapeutic insight who can deliver state-of-the-art healthcare. Still others need a veterinary facility that is open evenings and weekends, is in close proximity or provides mobile veterinary services to accommodate their schedules; these people may not much mind that their dogs might see different veterinarians on each visit. Just as we have different reasons for selecting our own healthcare professionals (e.g., covered by insurance plan, expert in field, convenient location, etc.), we should not expect that there is a one-size-fits-all recommendation for selecting a veterinarian and veterinary practice. The best advice is to be honest in your assessment of what you expect from a veterinary practice and to conscientiously research the options in your area. You will quickly appreciate that not all veterinary practices are the same, and you will be happiest with one that truly meets your needs.

There is another point to be considered in the selection of veterinary services. Not that long ago, a single veterinarian would attempt to manage all medical and surgical issues as they arose. That was often problematic,

Giant breeds like the Tibetan Mastiff have specific nutritional and healthcare needs related to their large size. Find a vet with large-dog experience who can provide your dog with the best care.

because veterinarians are trained in many species and many diseases, and it was just impossible for general veterinary practitioners to be experts in every species, every breed, every field and every ailment. However, just as in the human healthcare fields, specialization has allowed general practitioners to concentrate on primary healthcare delivery, especially wellness and the prevention of infectious diseases, and to utilize a network of specialists to assist in the management of conditions that require specific expertise and experience. Thus there are now many types of veterinary specialists, including dermatologists, cardiologists, ophthalmologists, surgeons, internists, oncologists, neurologists, behaviorists, criticalists and others to help primary-care veterinarians deal with complicated medical challenges. In most cases, specialists see cases referred by

primary-care veterinarians, make diagnoses and set up management plans. From there, the animals' ongoing care is returned to their primary-care veterinarians. This important team approach to your pet's medical-care needs has provided opportunities for advanced care and an unparalleled level of quality to be delivered. Additionally, homeopathic, naturopathic, chiropractic and acupuncture veterinary methods have been used successfully in conjunction with conventional veterinary care.

With all of the opportunities for your Tibetan Mastiff to receive high-quality veterinary medical care, there is another topic that needs to be addressed at the same time—cost. It's been said that you can have excellent healthcare or inexpensive healthcare, but never both; this is as true in veterinary medicine as it is in human medicine. While veterinary costs are a fraction of what the same services cost in the human healthcare arena, it is still difficult to deal with unanticipated medical costs, especially since they can easily creep into hundreds or even thousands of dollars if specialists or emergency services become involved. However, there are ways of managing these risks. The easiest is to buy pet health insurance and realize that its foremost purpose

HOT SPOTS

TMs are more prone to hot spots when in full coat, during a rainy season and especially in warmer, humid climates. Mild hot spots are often treated by cleaning them with peroxide and then applying cornstarch or a medicated antifungal spray powder to dry the area; this is done to avoid a staph infection. Moderate and severe hot spots need to be treated by your veterinarian.

A roll in the snow to scratch an itch feels great to the grinning Annie.

is not to cover routine healthcare visits but rather to serve as an umbrella for those rainy days when your pet needs medical care and you don't want to worry about whether or not you can afford that care.

Pet insurance policies are very cost-effective (and very inexpensive by human health-insurance standards), but make sure that you buy the policy long before you intend to use it (preferably starting in puppyhood, because coverage will exclude pre-existing conditions) and that you are actually buying an indemnity insurance plan from an insurance company that is regulated by your state or province. Many insurance policy look-alikes are actually discount clubs that are redeemable only at specific locations and for specific services. An indemnity plan covers your pet at almost all veterinary, specialty and emergency practices and is an excellent way to manage your pet's ongoing healthcare needs.

VACCINATIONS AND INFECTIOUS DISEASES

There has never been an easier time to prevent a variety of infectious diseases in your dog, but the advances we've made in veterinary medicine come with a price—choice. Now while it may seem that this choice is a good thing (and it is), it also has never been more difficult for the pet

COMMON INFECTIOUS DISEASES

Let's discuss some of the diseases that create the need for vaccination in the first place. Following are the major canine infectious diseases and a simple explanation of each.

Rabies: A devastating viral disease that can be fatal in dogs and people. In fact, vaccination of dogs and cats is an important public-health measure to create a resistant animal buffer population to protect people from contracting the disease. Vaccination schedules are determined on a government level and are not optional for pet owners; rabies vaccination is required by law in all 50 states and Canadian provinces.

Parvovirus: A severe, potentially life-threatening disease that is easily transmitted between dogs. There are four strains of the virus, but it is believed that there is significant "cross-protection" between strains that may be included in individual vaccines.

Distemper: A potentially severe and life-threatening disease with a relatively high risk of exposure, especially in certain regions. In very high-risk distemper environments, young pups may be vaccinated with human measles vaccine, a related virus that offers cross-protection when administered at four to ten weeks of age.

Hepatitis: Caused by canine adenovirus type 1 (CAV-1), but since vaccination with the causative virus has a higher rate of adverse effects, cross-protection is derived from the use of adenovirus type 2 (CAV 2), a cause of respiratory disease and one of the potential causes of canine cough. Vaccination with CAV-2 provides long-term immunity against hepatitis, but relatively less protection against respiratory infection.

Canine cough: Also called tracheobronchitis, actually a fairly complicated result of viral and bacterial offenders; therefore, even with vaccination, protection is incomplete. Wherever dogs congregate, canine cough will likely be spread among them. Intranasal vaccination with *Bordetella* and parainfluenza is the best safeguard, but the duration of immunity does not appear to be very long, typically a year at most. These are non-core vaccines, but vaccination is sometimes mandated by boarding kennels, obedience classes, dog shows and other places where dogs congregate to try to minimize spread of infection.

Leptospirosis: A potentially fatal disease that is more common in some geographic regions. It is capable of being spread to humans. The disease varies with the individual "serovar," or strain, of *Leptospira* involved. Since there does not appear to be much cross-protection between serovars, protection is only as good as the likelihood that the serovar in the vaccine is the same as the one in the pet's local environment. Problems with *Leptospira* vaccines are that protection does not last very long, side effects are not uncommon and a large percentage of dogs (perhaps 30%) may not respond to vaccination.

Borrelia burgdorferi: The cause of Lyme disease, the risk of which varies with the geographic area in which the pet lives and travels. Lyme disease is spread by deer ticks in the eastern US and western black-legged ticks in the western part of the country, and the risk of exposure is high in some regions. Lameness, fever and inappetence are most commonly seen in affected dogs. The extent of protection from the vaccine has not been conclusively demonstrated.

Coronavirus: This disease has a high risk of exposure, especially in areas where dogs congregate, but it typically causes only mild to moderate digestive upset (diarrhea, vomiting, etc.). Vaccines are available, but the duration of protection is believed to be relatively short and the effectiveness of the vaccine in preventing infection is considered low.

There are many other vaccinations available, including those for *Giardia* and canine adenovirus-1. While there may be some specific indications for their use, and local risk factors to be considered, they are not widely recommended for most dogs.

owner (or the vet) to make an informed decision about the best way to protect pets through vaccination.

Years ago, it was just accepted that puppies got a starter series of vaccinations and then annual "boosters" throughout their lives to keep them protected. As more and more vaccines became available, consumers wanted the convenience of having all of that protection in a single injection. The result was "multivalent" vaccines that crammed a lot of protection into a single syringe. The manufacturers' recommendations were to give the vaccines annually, and this was a simple enough protocol to follow. However, as veterinary medicine has become more sophisticated and we have started looking more at healthcare quandaries rather than convenience, it became necessary to reevaluate the situation and deal with some tough questions. It is important to realize that whether or not to use a particular vaccine depends on the risk of contracting the disease against which it protects, the severity of the disease if it is contracted, the duration of immunity provided by the vaccine, the safety of the

As inquisitive as 18-month-old Buddha is, he doesn't know much about his healthcare. It's up to you to make sure that your TM stays properly cared for, healthy and happy.

product and the needs of the individual animal. In a very general sense, rabies, distemper, hepatitis and parvovirus are considered core vaccine needs, while parainfluenza, *Bordetella bronchiseptica*, leptospirosis, coronavirus and borreliosis (Lyme disease) are considered non-core needs and best reserved for animals that demonstrate reasonable risk of contracting the diseases.

Dr. W. Jean Dodd's vaccination protocol is recommended by many Tibetan Mastiff breeders for the breed's sensitive system. Your vet will need to be made aware that a Tibetan Mastiff must never be casually medicated or sedated. The breed is sensitive to vaccines, anesthetics and chemicals.

NEUTERING/SPAYING

Sterilization procedures (neutering for males/spaying for females) are meant to accomplish several purposes. While the underlying premise is to address the risk of pet overpopulation, there are also some medical and behavioral benefits to the surgeries as well. For females, spaying prior to the first estrus (heat cycle) leads to a marked reduction in the risk of mammary cancer and other serious female health problems. There also will be no manifesta-

tions of "heat" to attract male dogs and no bleeding in the house. For males, there is prevention of testicular cancer and a reduction in the risk of prostate problems. In both sexes there may be some limited reduction in aggressive behaviors toward other dogs, and some diminishing of urine marking, roaming and mounting.

While neutering and spaying do indeed prevent animals from contributing to pet overpopulation, even no-cost and low-cost neutering options have not eliminated the problem. Perhaps one of the main reasons for this is that individuals that intentionally breed their dogs and those that allow their animals to run at large are the main causes of unwanted offspring. Also, animals in shelters are often there because they were abandoned or relinquished, not because they came from unplanned matings. Neutering/spaying is important, but it should be considered in the context of the real causes of animals' ending up in shelters and eventually being euthanized.

One of the important considerations regarding neutering is that it is a surgical procedure. This sometimes gets lost in discussions of low-cost procedures and commoditization of the process. In females, spaying is specifically referred to as an ovariohysterectomy. In this procedure, a midline incision is made in the abdomen and the entire uterus and both ovaries are surgically removed. While this is a

Eighteen-month-old King Kong, keeping a watchful eye while taking a rest. If you had to grow this much, you'd need to rest too!

major invasive surgical procedure, it usually has few complications because it is typically performed on healthy young animals. However, it is major surgery, as any woman who has had a hysterectomy will attest.

In males, neutering has traditionally referred to castration, which involves the surgical removal of both testicles. While still a significant piece of surgery, there is not the abdominal exposure that is required in the female surgery. In addition, there is now a chemical sterilization option, in which a solution is injected into each testicle, leading to atrophy of the sperm-producing cells. This can typically be done under sedation rather than full anesthesia. This is a relatively new approach, and there are no long-term clinical studies yet available.

The traditional thinking for neutering/spaying has always been to do so around six months of age, although new procedures are done in animals as young as eight weeks old before puppies go to their new homes. Recent health findings show that dogs and bitches benefit from being neutered/spayed later, to allow for natural, healthy, hormonally-based growth and development. Any TM female designated as "not for breeding" should be spayed by eight months old, and males neutered only when sexually aggressive behavior becomes problematic, as more health-related issues are found later in life in neutered males.

S.E.M. BY DR. DENNIS KUNKEL, UNIVERSITY OF HAWAII

A scanning electron micrograph of a dog flea, *Ctenocephalides canis*, on dog hair.

warmth of the animals' bodies, movement and exhaled carbon dioxide. However, when they first emerge from their cocoons, they orient towards light; thus when an animal passes between a flea and the light source, casting a shadow, the flea pounces and starts to feed. If the animal turns out to be a dog or cat, the reproductive cycle continues. If the flea lands on another type of animal, including a

EXTERNAL PARASITES

FLEAS

Fleas have been around for millions of years and, while we have better tools now for controlling them than at any time in the past, there still is little chance that they will end up on an endangered species list. Actually, they are very well adapted to living on our pets, and they continue to adapt as we make advances.

The female flea can consume 15 times her weight in blood during active reproduction and can lay as many as 40 eggs a day. These eggs are very resistant to the effects of insecticides. They hatch into larvae, which then mature and spin cocoons. The immature fleas reside in this pupal stage until the time is right for feeding. This pupal stage is also very resistant to the effects of insecticides, and pupae can last in the environment without feeding for many months. Newly emergent fleas are attracted to animals by the

FLEA PREVENTION FOR YOUR TIBETAN MASTIFF

- Any product used to eliminate parasites must be used with extreme caution due to the Tibetan Mastiff's more primitive and sensitive system. The vet must keep in mind the TM's sensitivity to chemicals.
- For dogs suffering from flea-bite dermatitis, a shampoo or topical insecticide treatment is required.
- Investigate safe ways to prevent fleas and ticks from lurking on your property.
- Using a flea comb, check the dog's coat regularly for any signs of parasites.
- Practice good housekeeping. Vacuum floors, carpets and furniture regularly, especially in the areas that the dog frequents, and wash the dog's bedding weekly.
- Follow up house-cleaning with carpet shampoos and sprays to rid the house of fleas at all stages of development. Insect growth regulators are the safest option.

person, the flea will bite but will then look for a more appropriate host. An emerging adult flea can survive without feeding for up to 12 months but, once it tastes blood, it can survive off its host for only 3 to 4 days.

It was once thought that fleas spend most of their lives in the environment, but we now know that fleas won't willingly jump off a dog unless leaping to another dog or when physically removed by brushing, bathing or other manipulation. Flea eggs, on the other hand, are shiny and smooth, and they roll off the animal and into the environment. The eggs, larvae and pupae then exist in the environment, but once the adult finds a susceptible animal, it's home sweet home until the flea is forced to seek refuge elsewhere.

Since adult fleas live on the animal and immature forms survive in the environment, a successful treatment plan must address all stages of the flea life cycle. There are now several safe and effective flea-control products that can be applied on a monthly basis. These include fipronil, imidacloprid, selamectin and permethrin (found in several formulations). Most of these products have significant flea-killing rates within 24 hours. However, none of them will control the immature forms in the environment. To accomplish this, there are a variety of insect growth regulators that can be sprayed into the

THE FLEA'S LIFE CYCLE

What came first, the flea or the egg? This age-old mystery is more difficult to comprehend than the actual cycle of the flea. Fleas usually live only about four months. A female can lay 2,000 eggs in her lifetime.

PHOTO BY CAROLINA BIOLOGICAL SUPPLY CO.

Egg

After ten days of rolling around your carpet or under your furniture, the eggs hatch into larvae, which feed on various and sundry debris. In days or

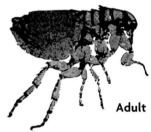

PHOTO BY CAROLINA BIOLOGICAL SUPPLY CO.

Larva

months, depending on the climate, the larvae spin cocoons and develop into the pupal or nymph stage, which quickly develop into fleas.

Pupa

These immature fleas must locate a host within 10 to 14 days or they will die. Only about 1% of the flea population exist as adult fleas, while the other 99% exist as eggs, larvae or pupae.

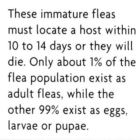

Adult

environment (e.g., pyriproxyfen, methoprene, fenoxycarb) as well as insect development inhibitors such as lufenuron that can be administered. These compounds have no effect on adult fleas, but they stop immature forms from developing into adults. In years gone by, we relied heavily on toxic insecticides (such as organophosphates, organochlorines and carbamates) to manage the flea problem, but today's options are not only much safer to use on our pets but also safer for the environment.

TICKS

Ticks are members of the spider class (arachnids) and are blood-sucking parasites capable of transmitting a variety of diseases, including Lyme disease, ehrlichiosis, babesiosis and Rocky Mountain spotted fever. It's easy to see ticks on your own skin, but it is more of a challenge when your furry companion is affected. Whenever you happen to be planning a stroll in a tick-infested area (especially forests, grassy or wooded areas or parks) be prepared to do a thorough inspection of your dog afterward to search for ticks. Finding ticks can be tricky, particularly in double-coated breeds like the TM, so be sure to

> ### TICK CONTROL
> Removal of underbrush and leaf litter and the thinning of trees in areas where tick control is desired are recommended. These actions remove the cover and food sources for small animals that serve as hosts for ticks. With continued mowing of grasses in these areas, the probability of ticks' surviving is further reduced. A variety of insecticide ingredients (e.g., resmethrin, carbaryl, permethrin, chlorpyrifos, dioxathion and allethrin) are registered for tick control around the home.

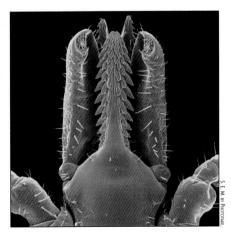

A scanning electron micrograph of the head of a female deer tick, *Ixodes dammini,* a parasitic tick that carries Lyme disease.

S. E. M. BY PHOTOTAKE

feel all the way down to the skin and spend time looking in the ears, between the toes and everywhere else where a tick might hide. Ticks need to be attached for 24–72 hours before they transmit most of the diseases that they carry, so you do have a window of opportunity for some preventive intervention.

Female ticks live to eat and breed. They can lay between 4,000 and 5,000 eggs and they die soon after. Males, on the other hand, live only to mate with the females and continue the process as long as they are able. Most ticks live on multiple hosts before parasitizing dogs. The immature forms typically reside on grass and shrubs, waiting for susceptible animals to walk by. The larvae and nymph stages typically feed on wildlife.

If only a few ticks are present on a dog, they can be plucked out, but it is important to remove the

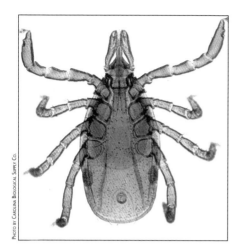

PHOTO BY CAROLINA BIOLOGICAL SUPPLY CO.

diseases caused by mites are referred to as "mange," and there are many different forms seen in dogs. These forms are very different from one another, each one warranting an individual description.

Sarcoptic mange, or scabies, is one of the itchiest conditions that affects dogs. The microscopic *Sarcoptes* mites burrow into the superficial layers of the skin and can drive dogs crazy with itchiness. They are also communicable to people, although they can't complete their reproductive cycle on people. In addition to being tiny, the mites also are often difficult to find when trying to make a diagnosis. Skin scrapings from multiple areas are examined microscopically but, even then, sometimes the mites cannot be found.

Deer tick, *Ixodes dammini*.

entire head and mouthparts, which may be deeply embedded in the skin. This is best accomplished with forceps designed especially for this purpose; fingers can be used but should be protected with rubber gloves, plastic wrap or at least a paper towel. The tick should be grasped as closely as possible to the animal's skin and should be pulled upward with steady, even pressure. Do not squeeze, crush or puncture the body of the tick or you risk exposure to any disease carried by that tick. Once the ticks have been removed, the sites of attachment should be disinfected. Your hands should then be washed with soap and water to further minimize risk of contagion. The tick should be disposed of in a container of alcohol or household bleach.

MITES
Mites are tiny arachnid parasites that parasitize the skin of dogs. Skin

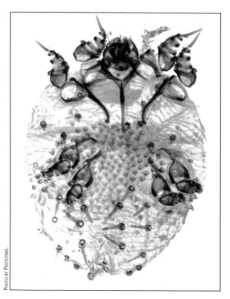

PHOTO BY PHOTOTAKE.

Sarcoptes scabiei, commonly known as the "itch mite."

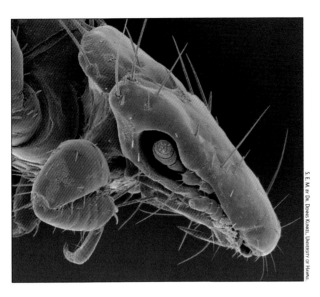

S.E.M. BY DR. DENNIS KUNKEL, UNIVERSITY OF HAWAII.

Micrograph of a dog louse, *Heterodoxus spiniger*. Female lice attach their eggs to the hairs of the dog. As the eggs hatch, the larval lice bite and feed on the blood. Lice can also feed on dead skin and hair. This feeding activity can cause hair loss and skin problems.

Illustration of *Demodex folliculoram*.

Fortunately, scabies is relatively easy to treat, and there are a variety of products that will successfully kill the mites. Since the mites can't live in the environment for very long without feeding, a complete cure is usually possible within four to eight weeks.

Cheyletiellosis is caused by a relatively large mite, which sometimes can be seen even without a microscope. Often referred to as "walking dandruff," this also causes itching, but not usually as profound as with scabies. While *Cheyletiella* mites can survive somewhat longer in the environment than scabies mites, they too are relatively easy to treat, being responsive to not only the medications used to treat scabies but also often to flea-control products.

Otodectes cynotis is the canine ear mite and is one of the more common causes of mange, especially in young dogs in shelters or pet stores. That's because the mites are typically present in large numbers and are quickly spread to nearby animals. The mites rarely do much harm but can be difficult to eradicate if the treatment regimen is not comprehensive. While many try to treat the condition with ear drops only, this is the most common cause of treatment failure. Ear drops cause the mites to simply move out of the ears and as far away as possible (usually to the base of the tail) until the insecticide levels in the ears drop to an acceptable level—then it's back to business as usual! The successful treatment of ear mites requires treating all animals in the household with a systemic insecticide, such as selamectin, or a combination of miticidal ear drops combined with whole-body flea-control preparations.

Demodicosis, sometimes referred to as red mange, can be one of the most difficult forms of mange to treat. Part of the problem has to do with the fact that the mites live in the hair follicles and they are relatively well shielded from topical and systemic products. The main issue, however, is that demodectic mange typically results only when there is some underlying process interfering with the

ILLUSTRATION BY PHOTOTAKE

dog's immune system.

Since *Demodex* mites are normal residents of the skin of mammals, including humans, there is usually a mite population explosion only when the immune system fails to keep the number of mites in check. In young animals, the immune deficit may be transient or may reflect an actual inherited immune problem. In older animals, demodicosis is usually seen only when there is another disease hampering the immune system, such as diabetes, cancer, thyroid problems or the use of immune-suppressing drugs. Accordingly, treatment involves not only trying to kill the mange mites but also discerning what is interfering with immune function and correcting it if possible.

Chiggers represent several different species of mite that don't parasitize dogs specifically, but do latch on to passersby and can cause irritation. The problem is most prevalent in wooded areas in the late summer and fall. Treatment is not difficult, as the mites do not complete their life cycle on dogs and are susceptible to a variety of miticidal products.

MOSQUITOES

Mosquitoes have long been known to transmit a variety of diseases to people, as well as just being biting pests during warm weather. They also pose a real risk to pets. Not only do they carry deadly heart-worms but recently there also has been much concern over their involvement with West Nile virus. While we can avoid heartworm with the use of preventive medications, there are no such preventives for West Nile virus. The only method of prevention in endemic areas is active mosquito control. Fortunately, most dogs that have been exposed to the virus only developed flu-like symptoms and, to date, there have not been the large number of reported deaths in canines as seen in some other species.

MOSQUITO REPELLENT

Low concentrations of DEET (less than 10%), found in many human mosquito repellents, have been safely used in dogs but, in these concentrations, probably give only about two hours of protection. DEET may be safe in these small concentrations, but since it is not licensed for use on dogs, there is no research proving its safety for dogs. Products containing permethrin give the longest-lasting protection, perhaps two to four weeks. As DEET is not licensed for use on dogs, and both DEET and permethrin can be quite toxic to cats, appropriate care should be exercised. Other products, such as those containing oil of citronella, also have some mosquito-repellent activity, but typically have a relatively short duration of action.

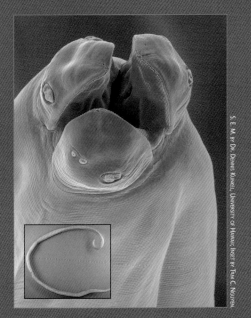

The ascarid roundworm *Toxocara canis*, showing the mouth with three lips. INSET: Photomicrograph of the roundworm *Ascaris lumbricoides*.

The hookworm *Ancylostoma caninum* infests the intestines of dogs. INSET: Note the row of hooks at the posterior end, used to anchor the worm to the intestinal wall.

INTERNAL PARASITES: WORMS

ASCARIDS

Ascarids are intestinal roundworms that rarely cause severe disease in dogs. Nonetheless, they are of major public health significance because they can be transferred to people. Sadly, it is children who are most commonly affected by the parasite, probably from inadvertently ingesting ascarid-contaminated soil. In fact, many yards and children's sandboxes contain appreciable numbers of ascarid eggs. So, while ascarids don't bite dogs or latch onto their intestines to suck blood, they do cause some nasty medical conditions in children and are best eradicated from our furry friends. Because pups can start passing ascarid eggs by three weeks of age, most parasite-control programs begin at two weeks of age and are repeated every two weeks until pups are eight weeks old. It is important to realize that bitches can pass ascarids to their pups even if they test negative prior to whelping. Accordingly, bitches are best treated at the same time as the pups.

HOOKWORMS

Unlike ascarids, hookworms do latch onto a dog's intestinal tract and can cause significant loss of blood and protein. Similar to ascarids, hookworms can be transmitted to humans, where they cause a condition known as cutaneous larval migrans. Dogs can become infected either by consuming the infective larvae or by the larvae's penetrating the skin directly. People most often get infected when they are lying on the ground (such as on a beach) and the larvae penetrate the skin. Yes, the larvae can penetrate through a beach blanket. Hookworms are typically susceptible to the same medications used to treat ascarids.

HEARTWORMS

Heartworm disease is caused by the parasite *Dirofilaria immitis* and is seen in dogs around the world. A member of the roundworm group, it is spread between dogs by the bite of an infected mosquito. The

WORM-CONTROL GUIDELINES

- Practice sanitary habits with your dog and home.
- Clean up after your dog and don't let him sniff or eat other dogs' droppings.
- Control insects and fleas in the dog's environment. Fleas, lice, cockroaches, beetles, mice and rats can act as hosts for various worms.
- Prevent dogs from eating uncooked meat, raw poultry and dead animals.
- Keep dogs and children from playing in sand and soil.
- Kennel dogs on cement or gravel; avoid dirt runs.
- Administer heartworm preventives regularly.
- Have your vet examine your dog's stools at your annual visits.
- Select a boarding kennel carefully so as to avoid contamination from other dogs or an unsanitary environment.
- Prevent dogs from roaming. Obey local leash laws.

Ascarid *Rhabditis*

Hookworm *Ancylostoma caninum*

Tapeworm *Dipylidium caninum*

Heartworm *Dirofilaria immitis*

PHOTO BY CAROLINA BIOLOGICAL SUPPLY CO.

PHOTO BY CAROLINA BIOLOGICAL SUPPLY CO.

PHOTO BY TAM C. NGUYEN

PHOTO BY TAM C. NGUYEN

mosquito injects infective larvae into the dog's skin with its bite, and these larvae develop under the skin for a period of time before making their way to the heart. There they develop into adults, which grow and create blockages of the heart, lungs and major blood vessels there. They also start producing offspring (microfilariae), and these microfilariae circulate in the bloodstream, waiting to hitch a ride when the next mosquito bites. Once in the mosquito, the microfilariae develop into infective larvae and the entire process is repeated.

When dogs get infected with heartworm, over time they tend

The dog tapeworm *Taenia pisiformis*.

S. E. M. by Dr. Dennis Kunkel, University of Hawaii.

to develop symptoms associated with heart disease, such as coughing, exercise intolerance and potentially many other manifestations. Diagnosis is confirmed by either seeing the microfilariae themselves in blood samples or using immunologic tests (antigen testing) to identify the presence of adult heartworms. Since antigen tests measure the presence of adult heartworms and microfilarial tests measure offspring produced by adults, neither are positive until six to seven months after the initial infection. However, the beginning of damage can occur by fifth-stage larvae as early as three months after infection. Thus it is possible for dogs to be harboring problem-causing larvae for up to three months before either type of test would identify an infection.

The good news is that there are great protocols available for preventing heartworm in dogs. Testing is critical in the process, and it is important to understand the benefits as well as the limitations of such testing. All dogs six months of age or older that have not been on continuous heartworm-preventive medication should be screened with microfilarial or antigen tests. For dogs receiving preventive medication, periodic antigen testing helps assess the

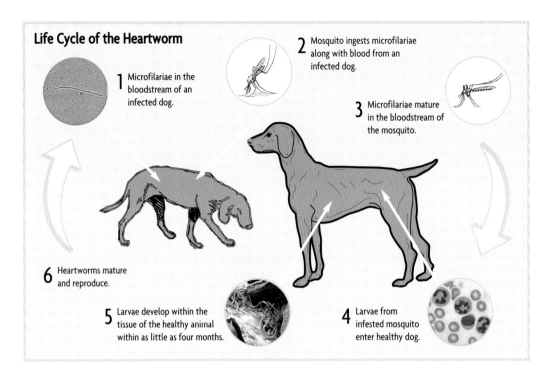

Life Cycle of the Heartworm

1 Microfilariae in the bloodstream of an infected dog.

2 Mosquito ingests microfilariae along with blood from an infected dog.

3 Microfilariae mature in the bloodstream of the mosquito.

4 Larvae from infested mosquito enter healthy dog.

5 Larvae develop within the tissue of the healthy animal within as little as four months.

6 Heartworms mature and reproduce.

effectiveness of the preventives. The American Heartworm Society guidelines suggest that annual retesting may not be necessary when owners have absolutely provided continuous heartworm prevention. Retesting on a two- to three-year interval may be sufficient in these cases. However, your veterinarian will likely have specific guidelines under which heartworm preventives will be prescribed, and many prefer to err on the side of safety and usually retest annually.

It is indeed fortunate that heartworm is relatively easy to prevent, because treatments can be as life-threatening as the disease itself. Treatment requires a two-step process that kills the adult heartworms first and then the microfilariae. Prevention is obviously preferable; this involves a once-monthly oral or topical treatment. The most common oral preventives include ivermectin (not suitable for some breeds), moxidectin and milbemycin oxime; the once-a-month topical drug selamectin provides heartworm protection in addition to flea, some types of tick and other parasite controls.

THE **ABC**S OF
Emergency Care

Abrasions
Clean wound with running water or 3% hydrogen peroxide. Pat dry with gauze and spray with antibiotic. Do not cover.

Animal Bites
Clean area with soap and saline solution or water. Apply pressure to any bleeding area. Apply antibiotic ointment. Identify animal and contact the vet.

Antifreeze Poisoning
Induce vomiting and take dog to the vet.

Bee Sting
Remove stinger and apply soothing lotion or cold compress; give antihistamine in proper dosage.

Bleeding
Apply pressure directly to wound with gauze or towel for five to ten minutes. If wound does not stop bleeding, wrap wound with gauze and adhesive tape.

Bloat/Gastric Torsion
Immediately take the dog to the vet or emergency clinic; phone from car. No time to waste.

Burns
Chemical: Bathe dog with water and pet shampoo. Rinse in saline solution. Apply antibiotic ointment.

Acid: Rinse with water. Apply one part baking soda, two parts water to affected area.

Alkali: Rinse with water. Apply one part vinegar, four parts water to affected area.

Electrical: Apply antibiotic ointment. Seek veterinary assistance immediately.

Choking
If the dog is on the verge of collapsing, wedge a solid object, such as the handle of a screwdriver, between molars on one side of the mouth to keep mouth open. Pull tongue out. Use long-nosed pliers or fingers to remove foreign object. Do not push the object down the dog's throat. For small or medium dogs, hold dog upside down by hind legs and shake firmly to dislodge foreign object.

Chlorine Ingestion
With clean water, rinse the mouth and eyes. Give the dog water to drink; contact the vet.

Constipation
Feed dog 2 tablespoons bran flakes with each meal. Encourage drinking water. Mix $1/4$-teaspoon mineral oil in dog's food. Contact vet if persists.

Diarrhea
Withhold food for 12 to 24 hours. Feed dog anti-diarrheal with eyedropper. When feeding resumes, feed one part boiled hamburger, one part plain cooked rice, $1/4$- to $3/4$-cup four times daily. Contact vet if persists longer than 24 hours.

Dog Bite
Snip away hair around puncture wound; clean with 3% hydrogen peroxide; apply tincture of iodine. Identify biting dog and contact the vet. If wound appears deep, take the dog to the vet.

Frostbite
Wrap the dog in a heavy blanket. Warm affected area with a warm bath for ten minutes. Red color to skin will return with circulation; if tissues are pale after 20 minutes, contact the vet.

Use a portable, durable container large enough to contain all items.

Heat Stroke
Partially submerge the dog in cold water; if no response within ten minutes, contact the vet.

Hot Spots
Mix 2 packets Domeboro® with 2 cups water. Saturate cloth with mixture and apply to hot spots for 15 to 30 minutes. Apply antibiotic ointment. Repeat every six to eight hours.

Poisonous Plants
Wash affected area with soap and water. Cleanse with alcohol. For foxtail/grass, apply antibiotic ointment. Contact the vet if plant is ingested.

Rat Poison Ingestion
Induce vomiting. Keep dog calm, maintain dog's normal body temperature (use blanket or heating pad). Get to the vet for antidote.

Shock
Keep the dog calm and warm; call for veterinary assistance.

Snake Bite
If possible, bandage the area and apply pressure. If the area is not conducive to bandaging, use ice to control bleeding. Get immediate help from the vet.

Tick Removal
Apply flea and tick spray directly on tick. Wait one minute. Using tweezers or wearing plastic gloves, apply constant pull while grasping tick's body. Apply antibiotic ointment.

Vomiting
Restrict dog's water intake; offer a few ice cubes. Withhold food for next meal. Contact vet if vomiting persists longer than 24 hours.

DOG OWNER'S FIRST-AID KIT
- ❑ Gauze bandages/swabs
- ❑ Adhesive and non-adhesive bandages
- ❑ Antibiotic powder
- ❑ Antiseptic wash
- ❑ Hydrogen peroxide 3%
- ❑ Antibiotic ointment
- ❑ Lubricating jelly
- ❑ Rectal thermometer
- ❑ Nylon muzzle
- ❑ Scissors and forceps
- ❑ Eyedropper
- ❑ Syringe
- ❑ Anti-bacterial/fungal solution
- ❑ Saline solution
- ❑ Antihistamine
- ❑ Cotton balls
- ❑ Nail clippers
- ❑ Screwdriver/pen knife
- ❑ Flashlight
- ❑ Emergency phone numbers

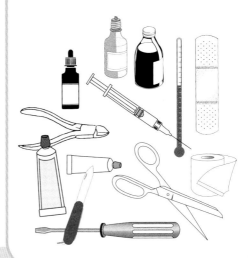

Is dog showing in your blood? Are you excited by the idea of gaiting your handsome Tibetan Mastiff around the ring to the thunderous applause of an enthusiastic audience? Are you certain that your beloved Tibetan Mastiff is flawless? You are not alone! Every loving owner thinks that his dog has no faults, or too few to mention. No matter how many times an owner reads the breed standard, he cannot find any faults in his aristocratic companion dog.

Good breeding, quality training, socialization and conditioning will give your Tibetan Mastiff every advantage in the show ring. This is Ayang-Salem Sundaram.

If this sounds like you, and if you are considering entering your Tibetan Mastiff in a dog show, here are some basic questions to ask yourself:

- Did you purchase a "show-quality" puppy from the breeder?
- Is your puppy old enough to show?
- Does the puppy exhibit correct show type for his breed?
- Does your puppy have any disqualifying faults?
- Is your Tibetan Mastiff registered with a national kennel club?
- How much time do you have to devote to training, grooming, conditioning and exhibiting your dog?
- Do you understand the rules and regulations of a dog show?
- Do you have time to learn how to show your dog properly?
- Do you have the financial resources to invest in showing your dog?
- Will you show the dog yourself or hire a professional handler (some organizations do not allow the use of professional handlers)?

AKC Best in Show judge Elaine Young with her 2005 national specialty Best of Breed winner Multi-Ch. Edgi Ganden Monge and owner/handler Richard W. Eichhorn.

- Do you have a vehicle that can accommodate your weekend trips to the dog shows?

Success in the show ring requires more than a pretty face, a waggy tail and a pocketful of liver. Even though dog shows can be exciting and enjoyable, the sport of conformation makes great demands on the exhibitors and the dogs. Winning exhibitors live for their dogs, devoting time and money to their dogs' presentation, conditioning and training. Very few novices, even those with good dogs, will find themselves in the winners' circle, though it does happen. Don't be disheartened, though. Every exhibitor began as a novice and worked his way up to the Group ring. It's the "working your way up" part that you must keep in mind.

Assuming that you have purchased a puppy of the correct type and quality for showing, let's begin to examine the world of showing and what's required to get started. Although the entry

---

WHAT DOES A TITLE SAY, REALLY?
Used with permission from and adapted by Penny White of the Tibetan Terrier Club of America.

A championship title, an obedience or agility title or a Canine Good Citizen® certificate—a title is a brag, yes, and sometimes a stepping stone to even higher competition, and it is undeniably a tribute to the dog that bears it. It is a way to honor the dog, a memorial that will remain in record and in memory. Although the dog doesn't know or care that his achievements have been noted, a title says many things in the world of humans, where such things count.

A title says your dog was intelligent, adaptable, skilled and good-natured. It says that your dog loved you enough to do what pleased you, however crazy it may have sometimes seemed to him! And a title says that you have loved your dog, that you loved to spend time with him because he was a good dog and that you believed in him enough to give him yet another chance when he failed (because rarely is a title attained quickly or easily!). It says that in the end, your faith in him was justified.

A title proves that you and your dog attained that special relationship enjoyed by so few in this world of disposable creatures and pleasures. This dog with a title was greatly loved, and he loved greatly in return. And when that dear, short life is over, the title remains as a memorial of the finest kind for a deserving friend. Volumes of praise in a small set of initials before or after his name. Like a university degree. A testament to toil and accomplishment.

A title is nothing less than true love and respect, given and received and recorded permanently.

fee into a dog show is nominal, there are lots of other hidden costs involved with "finishing" your Tibetan Mastiff, that is, making him a champion. Things like equipment, travel, training and conditioning all cost money. A more serious campaign will include fees for a professional handler, (although some organi-zations, like the UKC, do not allow professional handlers) boarding, cross-country travel and advertising. Top-winning show dogs can represent a very considerable investment—over $100,000 has been spent in campaigning some dogs.

Many owners, on the other hand, enter their "average" Tibetan Mastiffs in dog shows for the fun and enjoyment of it. Dog showing makes an absorbing hobby, with many rewards for dogs and owners alike. If you're having fun, meeting other people who share your interests and enjoying the overall experience, you likely will catch the "bug." Once the dog-show bug bites, its effects can last a lifetime; it's certainly much better than a deer tick! Soon you will be envisioning yourself in the center ring, competing for the presti-gious Best in Show cup.

The author is going over a line-up of Tibetan Mastiffs while judging at a recent dog show.

GETTING STARTED IN CONFORMATION

Visiting a dog show as a spectator is a great place to start. Pick up the show catalog to find out what time your breed is being shown, who is judging the breed and in which ring the classes will be held. To start, Tibetan Mastiffs compete against other Tibetan Mastiffs, and the winner is selected as Best of Breed by the judge. This is the procedure for each breed. At a group show, all of the Best of Breed winners go on to compete for Group One (first place) in their respective groups. For example, all Best of Breed winners in a given group compete against each other; this is done for all of the breed groups. Finally, all group winners go head to head in the ring for the Best in Show award.

What most spectators don't understand is the basic idea of conformation. A dog show is often

Breeders will often assess their young pups and decide which ones to show.

referred to as a "conformation" show. This means that the judge should decide how each dog stacks up (conforms) to the breed standard for his given breed: how well does this Tibetan Mastiff conform to the ideal representative detailed in the standard? Ideally, this is what happens. In reality, however, this ideal often gets slighted as the judge compares Tibetan Mastiff #1 to Tibetan Mastiff #2. Again, the ideal is that each dog is judged based on his merits in comparison to his breed standard, not in comparison to the other dogs in the ring. It is easier for judges to compare dogs of the same breed to decide which they think is the better specimen; in the Group and

Best in Show ring, however, it is very difficult to compare one breed to another, like apples to oranges. Thus the dog's conformation to the breed standard—not to mention advertising dollars and good handling—is essential to success in conformation shows. The dog described in the standard is the perfect dog of that breed, and breeders keep their eye on the standard when they choose which dogs to breed, hoping to get closer and closer to the ideal with each litter.

Another good first step for the novice is to join a dog club. You will be astonished by the many and different kinds of dog clubs in the country, with about 5,000 clubs holding events every year. Most clubs require that prospective new members present two letters of recommendation from existing members. Perhaps you've made some friends visiting a show held by a particular club and you would like to join that club. Dog clubs may specialize in a single breed, like a regional Tibetan Mastiff club, or in a specific pursuit, such as obedience or another type of competition. There are all-breed clubs for all dog enthusiasts; they sponsor special training days, seminars on topics like grooming or handling or lectures on breeding or canine genetics. There are also clubs that specialize in certain types of dogs, like molossers or rare breeds.

A parent club is the national organization, sanctioned by a national kennel club, which promotes and safeguards its breed in the country. The American Kennel Club (AKC) parent club is the American Tibetan Mastiff Association, which was formed in 1974 and can be contacted on the Internet at www.tibetanmastiff.org. The parent club for the United Kennel Club is the Tibetan Mastiff Club of America, which was formed in 1974 and can be contacted on the Internet at www.tmcamerica.org. Parent clubs hold annual national specialty shows, usually in different cities

each year, in which many of the country's top dogs, handlers and breeders gather to compete. At a specialty show, only members of a single breed are invited to participate. For more information about breed and dog clubs in your area, contact the AKC, the UKC or one of the national TM clubs.

AKC SHOWING

CONFORMATION
Three kinds of conformation shows are offered by the AKC. There is the all-breed show, in which all AKC-recognized breeds can compete; the specialty show, which is for one breed only and usually sponsored by the breed's parent club and the group show, for all breeds in one of the AKC's seven groups. As of January 2007, the Tibetan Mastiff has been part of the Working Group.

For a dog to become an AKC champion of record, the dog must earn 15 points at shows. The points must be awarded by at least three different judges and must include two "majors" under different judges. A "major" is a three-, four- or five-point win, and the number of points per win is determined by the number of dogs competing in the show on that day. (Dogs that are absent or are excused are not counted.) The number of points that are awarded varies from breed to breed. More dogs are needed to

FOR MORE INFORMATION...
For reliable up-to-date information about registration, dog shows and other canine competitions, contact one of the national registries by mail or via the Internet.

American Kennel Club
5580 Centerview Dr., Raleigh, NC 27606-3390
www.akc.org

United Kennel Club
100 E. Kilgore Road, Kalamazoo, MI 49002
www.ukcdogs.com

Canadian Kennel Club
89 Skyway Ave., Suite 100, Etobicoke, Ontario
M9W 6R4 Canada
www.ckc.ca

American Rare Breed Association
9921 Frank Tippett Road
Cheltenham, MD 20623
www.arba.org

attain a major in more popular breeds, and fewer dogs are needed in less popular breeds. Yearly, the AKC evaluates the number of dogs in competition in each division (there are 14 divisions in all, based on geography) and may or may not change the numbers of dogs required for each number of points in a given breed.

Only one dog and one bitch of each breed can win points at a given show. There are no "co-ed" classes except for champions of record. Dogs and bitches do not compete against each other until they are champions. Dogs that are not champions (referred to as "class dogs") compete in one of six classes. The class in which a dog is entered depends on age and previous show wins. First there is the Puppy Class (usually divided further into classes for 6- to 9-month-olds and 9- to 12-month-olds); then there is the 12- to 18-Months Class; next is the Novice Class (for dogs that have no points toward their championships and whose only first-place wins have come in the Puppy Class or the Novice Class, the latter class limited to three first places); then there is the American-bred Class (for dogs bred in the US); the Bred-by-Exhibitor Class (for dogs handled by their breeders or by immediate family members of their breeders) and the Open Class (for any non-champions). Any dog may enter the Open Class, regardless of age or win history, but to be competitive the dog should be older and have ring experience.

Proper training of your show puppy can have great rewards. Here is Drakyi Aura of Simba at Dawa winning Best of Breed Puppy at the 2006 TMCA national specialty.

The TM's debut in the AKC Miscellaneous Class at the Palm Springs Kennel Club show in January 2005.

The judge at the show begins judging the male dogs in the Puppy Class(es) and proceeds through the other classes. The judge awards first through fourth place in each class. The first-place winners of each class then compete with one another in the Winners Class to determine Winners Dog. The judge then starts over with the bitches, beginning with the Puppy Class(es) and proceeding up to the Winners Class to award Winners Bitch, just as he did with the dogs. A Reserve Winners Dog and Reserve Winners Bitch are also selected; they could be awarded the points in the case of a disqualification.

The Winners Dog and Winners Bitch are the two that are awarded the points for their breed. They then go on to compete with any champions of record (often called "specials") of their breed that are entered in the show. The champions may be dogs or bitches; in this class, all are shown together. The judge reviews the Winners Dog and Winners Bitch along with all of the champions to select the Best of Breed winner. The Best of Winners is selected between the Winners Dog and Winners Bitch; if one of these two is selected Best of Breed as well, he or she is automatically determined Best of Winners. Lastly, the judge selects Best of Opposite Sex to the Best of Breed winner. The Best of Breed winner then goes on to the group competition.

At a group or all-breed show, the Best of Breed winners from each breed are divided into their respective groups to compete against one another for Group One through Group Four. Group One (first place) is awarded to the dog that best lives up to the ideal for his breed as described in the standard. A group judge, therefore, must have a thorough working knowledge of many breed standards. After placements have been made in each group, the seven Group One winners (from the Working Group, Toy Group, Hound Group, etc.) compete against each other for the top honor, Best in Show.

There are different ways to find out about dog shows in your area. The American Kennel Club's monthly magazine, the *American Kennel Gazette* is accompanied by the *Events Calendar*; this magazine is available through subscription. You can also look on the AKC's and your parent club's websites for information and check the event listings in your local newspaper.

Your Tibetan Mastiff must be six months of age or older and registered with the AKC in order to be entered in AKC-sanctioned shows in which there are classes for the Tibetan Mastiff. Your Tibetan Mastiff also must not possess any disqualifying faults and must be sexually intact. The reason for the latter is simple: dog shows are the proving grounds to determine which dogs and bitches are worthy of being bred. If they cannot be bred, that defeats the purpose! If you have spayed or neutered your dog, however, there are many AKC events other than conformation, such as obedience trials, agility trials and the Canine Good Citizen® Program, in which you and your Tibetan Mastiff can participate.

From two World-Show-winning parents herself, Loka gets the finishing touches for her AKC show debut.

OBEDIENCE TRIALS

Mrs. Helen Whitehouse Walker, a Standard Poodle fancier, can be credited with introducing obedience trials to the United States. In the 1930s she designed a series of exercises based on those of the Associated Sheep, Police, Army Dog Society of Great Britain. These exercises were intended to evaluate the working relationship between dog and owner. Since those early days of the sport in the US, obedience trials have grown more and more popular, and now more than 2,000 trials each year attract over 100,000 dogs and their owners. Any dog registered with the AKC, regardless of neutering or other disqualifications that would preclude entry in conformation competition, can participate in obedience trials.

There are three levels of difficulty in obedience competition. The first (and easiest) level is the Novice, in which dogs can earn the Companion Dog (CD) title. The intermediate level is the Open level, in which the Companion Dog Excellent (CDX) title is awarded. The advanced level is the Utility level, in which dogs compete for the Utility Dog (UD) title. Classes at each level are further divided into "A" and "B," with "A" for beginners and "B" for those with more experience. In order to win a title at a given level, a dog must earn three "legs." A "leg" is accomplished when a dog scores 170 or higher (200 is a perfect score). The scoring system gets a little trickier when you understand that a dog must score more than 50% of the points available for each exercise in order to actually earn the points. Available points for each exercise range between 20 and 40.

A dog must complete different exercises at each level of obedience. The Novice exercises are the easiest, with the Open and finally the Utility levels progressing in difficulty. Examples

of Novice exercises are on- and off-lead heeling, a figure-8 pattern, performing a recall (or come), long sit and long down and standing for examination. In the Open level, the Novice-level exercises are required again, but this time without a leash and for longer durations. In addition, the dog must clear a broad jump, retrieve over a jump and drop on recall. In the Utility level, the exercises are quite difficult, including executing basic commands based on hand signals, following a complex heeling pattern, locating articles based on scent discrimination and completing jumps at the handler's direction.

Once he's earned the UD title, a dog can go on to win the prestigious title of Utility Dog Excellent

Owned by Debbie Parsons, Multi-Ch. Drakyi Loki takes the prestigious 2006 national specialty Best of Breed award with handler Michael Brantley.

(UDX) by winning "legs" in ten shows. Additionally, Utility Dogs who win "legs" in Open B and Utility B earn points toward the lofty title of Obedience Trial Champion (OTCh.). Established in 1977 by the AKC, this title requires a dog to earn 100 points as well as 3 first places in a combination of Open B and Utility B classes under 3 different judges. The "brass ring" of obedience competition is the AKC's National Obedience Invitational. This is an exclusive competition for only the cream of the obedience crop. In order to qualify for the invitational, a dog must be ranked in either the top 25 all-breeds in obedience or in the top 3 for his breed in obedience. The title at stake here is that of National Obedience Champion (NOC).

THE UNITED KENNEL CLUB

Rare breeds in the United States have many opportunities to compete in both conformation and other events. A glance at the United Kennel Club (UKC) website (www.ukcdogs.com) tells us that the UKC is America's second oldest and second largest all-breed dog registry, attracting around 250,000 registrations each year. Chauncey Z. Bennett founded the UKC in 1898 with an aim to support the "total dog," meaning a dog that possesses quality in physical conformation and performance alike. With that in mind, the UKC sponsors competitive events that emphasize this "total dog" aspect. Along with traditional conformation shows, the UKC's performance events encompass just about every skill that one could imagine in a dog! The website

At the TMCA 2006 national specialty weekend in Sacramento, California, Sue Elworthy and Thor relax before the judging begins.

goes on to say, "As a departure from registries that place emphasis on a dog's looks, UKC events are designed for dogs that look and perform equally well." The UKC does host conformation shows, the traditional "dog shows."

The breed standards recognized by the UKC are either adopted from those of Europe's canine registry, the Fédération Cynologique Internationale (FCI), or submitted by the American breed club and then revised and adopted by the UKC. At many shows, handlers will receive verbal "critiques" of their dogs; these critiques may always be requested if not given automatically. This critique details a dog's comparison to the breed standard, and the judge also will explain why he placed each dog as he did.

UKC dog shows may be held for one breed only, several breeds or all breeds. UKC shows are arranged differently from the conformation shows of other organizations. Entries are restricted by age, and you cannot show your dog in a class other than his correct age class. When you compete for championship points, you may enter Puppy (6–12 months), Junior (1–2 years), Senior (2–3 years) or Adult (3 years and older). You may also enter the Breeder/Handler Class, where dogs of all ages compete,

Following their Reserve Best in Show win at the Canadian Molosser Association Specialty is Junior Handler Alex Elworthy and his dog Guardian's Meili of Everest.

but the dog must be handled by his breeder or a member of the breeder's immediate family. The winners of each class compete for Best Male or Best Female. These two dogs then compete for Best of Winners; the dog who is given this award will go on to compete for Best of Breed. Best of Breed competition includes the Best of Winners and dogs that have earned Champion and Grand Champion titles. Earning Best Male or Best Female, as long as there is competition, is considered a "major."

Once a dog has earned 3 "majors" and accumulated 100 points, he is considered a UKC champion. What this means is that the dog is now ready to compete for the title of Grand Champion,

A beautiful portrait of Multi-Ch. Wangdi's Fuso Spit'n Imag O Jack, one of the top-winning TMs of all time, owner/handled by Audrey Lee.

which is equivalent to an AKC championship. To earn the Grand Champion title, a dog must compete with a minimum of two other dogs who are also champions. The dog must win this class, called the Champion of Champions Class, five times under three different judges. In rare breeds, it is difficult to assemble a class of champions, so the UKC Grand Champion title is truly a prestigious one. Once a dog has earned the Grand Champion title,

he can continue to compete for Top Ten, but there are no further titles to earn. "Top Ten" refers to the ten dogs in each breed that have won the most points in a given year. These dogs compete in a Top Ten invitational competition annually.

The breeds recognized by the UKC are divided into groups. The Tibetan Mastiff competes in Group 1, Guardian Dogs, which consists of flock guard breeds and mastiff breeds. Depending on the show-giving club, group competition may or may not be offered. A group must have a minimum of five breeds entered in order for group competition to take place. If group competition is offered, Best in Show consists of the group winners. If there is no group competition, then all Best of Breed dogs go into the ring at the same time to compete for Best in Show. This can be a large number of dogs and thus can be very interesting, to say the least!

Aside from the variations already presented, UKC shows differ from other dog shows in one very significant way: no professional handlers are allowed to show dogs, except for those dogs they own themselves. UKC shows create an atmosphere that is owner-friendly, relaxed and genuinely fun. Bait in the ring is allowed at the discretion of the judge, but throwing the bait, dropping it on the floor or other

Bohemia Sirague Orson and Lafahhs Lamto pose for their Best of Breed and Best of Opposite Sex wins.

"handler tricks" will get an owner excused from the ring in a big hurry.

In addition to dog shows, the UKC offers many, many more venues for dogs and their owners, in keeping with its mission of promoting the "total dog." UKC obedience events test the training of dogs as they perform a series of prescribed exercises at the commands of their handlers. There are several levels of competition, ranging from basic commands such as "sit," "come" and "heel," to advanced exercises like scent discrimination and directed retrieves over jumps, based on the dog's level of accomplishment. The classes are further delineated by the experience of the handler.

UKC obedience differs from AKC obedience in many respects. Even at the most basic levels, the dogs are expected to "honor" other dogs who are working. In other words, the "honoring" dog must be placed in a down/stay while his owner leaves the ring and moves out of sight. The dog must remain in the down/stay position while the working dog goes through the heeling exercises.

OTHER RARE-BREED ORGANIZATIONS

We have mentioned some of the organizations that offer registration and competitive events. The availability of these events depends on geography. The IABCA (International All-Breed Canine Association of America) holds conformation shows under FCI rules. This club offers both American and international judges at all of their shows. Most of their events are held in the western US, but now also are offered in both the Midwest and Florida.

As with UKC shows, IABCA shows divide dogs by age. Dogs are considered "puppies" up to 18 months of age for large breeds

Sollay readies for examination and evaluation, giving the judge her best expression and show stance.

Loki shows the sound movement that made him the first all-breed Miscellaneous Best in Show in AKC history.

In order for a dog to earn a championship, he must receive three V-1 ratings. Each dog is given a written critique during the class. The judge will ask the handler to stand near the judges' table and will either make notes or dictate to the ring steward as he compares your dog to the standard. A handler can listen while the judge does this and often the judge will ask questions, especially of handlers showing rare-breed dogs. It is a very interesting and educational procedure, to say the least. Rare breeds can earn a championship without competing against other dogs, because the dog is always competing against the breed standard. There are times when no dog in a breed receives a V-1 if none is of sufficient quality to warrant such a rating.

and up to 15 months of age for smaller breeds. You cannot enter your dog in any class except the appropriate class for his age. After puppyhood, you can enter your dog in the adult class. Once your dog has earned his championship, he goes on to compete for various ranks of champion, of which there are too many to enumerate here. There are fun classes as well, one of which is "Best Rare Breed in Show." This class is only offered on the Sunday of a show weekend, and only those dogs earning the highest award possible in their classes may enter (Best Puppy, Best of Breed).

Another organization, the American Rare Breed Association (ARBA), holds shows across the country, although not in great numbers. In ARBA competition, as in IABCA competition, a dog can win points and earn his championship by showing against the standard, not necessarily against other dogs. ARBA's Cherry Blossom show, held annually in Washington, DC each spring, draws a handsome entry.

A show-giving group called Rarities, Inc. also has arrived on the scene in the United States and Canada. This group is dedicated to the support of ancient and rare breeds. To obtain a championship, a dog requires 15 points. Of these 15 points, the dog must have attained 2 "majors" of at least 3 points under 2 different judges; further, the total of 15 points must have been obtained under 3 different judges. Shows with double points awarded count toward both the American and Canadian championship. To earn the International Championship, the dog must win both the American and Canadian championships. The Grand Champion title is earned by defeating 15 other Rarities or FCI champions. Grand Champions (not pending Grand Champions) may compete for the title Supreme Grand Champion, which is earned by defeating 15 other Rarities Grand Champions. In Rarities shows, as in AKC and UKC shows, a dog must defeat other dogs in order to earn a championship. One of the unique things about Rarities, Inc. is that all Working Group breeds (which includes the TM) must also pass a temperament test.

A fully mature Multi-Ch. Edgi Ganden Monge, in show coat and condition, displaying his winning Best in Show form.

INDEX

My Tibetan Mastiff

PUT YOUR PUPPY'S FIRST PICTURE HERE

Dog's Name _____

Date _____ Photographer _____